FIX YOUR
LIFE
NOW!

To Anne and Ian

FIX YOUR LIFE NOW!

DUNCAN GOODHEW
& VICTORIA HISLOP

Vermilion
LONDON

3 5 7 9 10 8 6 4 2

Text © Duncan Goodhew & Victoria Hislop 2001

Duncan Goodhew and Victoria Hislop have asserted their right to be
identified as the authors of this work under the Copyright, Designs
and Patents Act 1988.

First published in the United Kingdom in 2001 by Vermillion
an imprint of Ebury Press
Random House
20 Vauxhall Bridge Road · London SW1V 2SA

The Random House Group Limited supports The Forest Stewardship
Council (FSC®), the leading international forest certification organisation.
Our books carrying the FSC label are printed on FSC® certified paper.
FSC is the only forest certification scheme endorsed by the leading
environmental organisations, including Greenpeace. Our
paper procurement policy can be found at
www.randomhouse.co.uk/environment

MIX
Paper from
responsible sources
FSC® C018072

A CIP catalogue record for this book is available from the British Library

ISBN 9780091948061

Design and illustrations by Lovelock & Co.

Printed and bound in Great Britain by Clays Ltd, St Ives plc

Contents

Preface

We'd all like to maintain the physique we had at 18 and the energy and drive we had at 21. Sadly, there's little chance of either. Even if your musical taste hasn't changed since the late 1970s (still cherish your heavy metal albums and occasionally perform in secret on air guitar?), your body almost certainly has and some of this change is inevitable. But not all of it – and there's no reason to accept an all-round decline without putting up a good fight! You can't turn back the clock but you can try to regain your youthful zest, avoid adrenalin addiction and minimise your decline in performance.

In this book, we give you an easy six-point plan to follow. Each step guides you towards a few changes that are small in themselves but will result in some radical improvements. We've listed some of the danger zones (SOS's) and thrown you a few life preservers – and at the end of each chapter there's a series of action points to help you form a template for continued change and improvement in your life.

If you don't relish the prospect of slipping into a pipe-and-slippers-by-the-fireside routine this side of your 60th birthday, this is the book which will give you back your energy and motivation. This is the book to FIX YOUR LIFE – NOW!

Introduction

The most important factor in your overall performance has to be your health. Without it, your life horizons will close in. But what is your definition of good health? Is it more than just freedom from coughs and colds? Getting through the month without a migraine? Or reaching retirement without suffering a coronary? Yes, these things are part of it, but it should be much, much more. My own definition of health is waking up on a daily basis with a genuine sense of energy and well-being. It is feeling that you are on top of everything in your life rather than that everything is on top of you – that you could leap out of bed in the morning and achieve anything at all you set your mind to.

A few years ago I attended the World Transplant Games and met a bunch of people who were so filled with zest and *joie de vivre* it took my breath away. These were people who had, through the miracles of modern medicine, been given a second chance. They were people for whom life really felt like a gift, on an hour-by-hour, day-by-day basis. Two guys particularly stood out. They had been operated on in a 'dominoes' transplant. One of them had needed a new lung which, to give an increased survival rate, includes transplanting a healthy heart, and the other was a patient who had then received that heart. During rehabilitation they became good friends and took up running together, on one occasion holding hands through the finishing line to win the 400 metres. On the rostrum, the lung transplant patient joked with the official 'You can give me both the gold medals – it was my heart that won his race!' These people experienced everything very intensely because they had been given that second chance. For them, life was always in full colour. It's an attitude we should all aspire to, especially since most of us will probably only have the one opportunity for life. This book will give you the framework to acquire this approach to life – without the risk and discomfort of major surgery! So read on.

If you think physical fitness is only important for athletes and football players think again. The benefits of exercise and paying attention to your body are immeasurable, not just in terms of making you stronger and giving you a longer life, but also in making you feel generally better on a day-by-day basis. **A six-pack stomach and bulging biceps are the traditional goals of exercise, but much more important are the feelings of contentment and control which are a guaranteed result.** As you get older it becomes increasingly important to put some work into looking after your body – and that includes making sure that it's kept nourished with the right fuel.

What was the male body designed for? Sitting in an office, staring at a computer screen and shifting bits of paper from one side of a desk to another is almost certainly not the answer. Far from it. As hunter-gatherers, men were engaged in a great deal of strenuous physical activity. Over the centuries the nature of our work has changed dramatically, but our bodies haven't altered to take this into account. No wonder we get fat, sluggish and bad-tempered if we spend all day hunched over a desk and all evening lying slumped in an armchair. In more primitive times the mind and body were largely used in equal measure. Now, for much of our lives, the body is underused, redundant even – so no wonder it starts to protest. Exercise is absolutely vital to your well-being and can play a big part in keeping you healthy into old age – I am continually inspired by my 95-year-old grandmother, who cycled until she was 86 and until 18 months ago walked three miles a day.

But exercise is only one of a set of tools which can make a big difference to your life.

The sedentary, but nevertheless stressful, lives which many of us lead can create a depressing chain of inevitabilities. Here are the consequences if you don't build some habits for healthy living into your life:

- You're too busy working
- So you don't eat properly
- So you feel tired and enervated
- So you don't bother to exercise
- So you lose your self-esteem
- So you eat for comfort
- So you get fat and unfit
- So your self-esteem drops even further
- So you lose confidence at work and in your relationships
- So you start to sink

If this sounds familiar – or perhaps you just recognise yourself in the first stages of the chain – now is the moment to start getting a grip on the situation.

A decade ago you probably had a great deal more energy – and more motivation and drive than you knew what to do with. But what a difference ten years can make. You are likely to be less fit than you were at 21 (unless you've worked very hard to sustain your fitness level), and even at that age it wasn't exactly healthy to skip breakfast, drown yourself in black coffee and chuck in the odd Mars bar for good measure until lunch (or even dinner) and then have a five-course blow-out with a bottle of red and two brandies. **The occasional game of five-a-side football, a monthly squash match and an annual cricket fixture at your old school may just about have sufficed as your exercise regime when you were 25,** but beyond that age treating your system like this can have really disastrous consequences. Without trying to depress you, it's no coincidence that Club 18–30 Holidays defines its target market so openly. You wouldn't be able to stay the pace. You really do move into a different bracket in the second part of your thirties – if you haven't already got the picture, youth is no longer on your side.

Your metabolic rate, for example, which determines how quickly your body uses energy, starts to slow down after you reach 35. An active man in the 18–30 age group, for example, will burn up around 3,000 calories a day, but at the age of around 36, his body will require only 2,800 calories a day. So if you continue to do the same amount of exercise and eat and drink in just the same way as you have since you were 18, it will really start to show up now – around the middle.

This change is accompanied by other equally unwelcome ones: you feel less energetic, your hair (if you still have any) starts to go grey and middle-age spread finally catches up with you. You're running out of notches on your belt and, yes, it is entirely in your imagination that the number of stairs to your office has increased, there's simply more of you to get to the top of them. If you've started taking the lift, then STOP as from tomorrow.

If your body weight is on the way up, the same is probably not true of your career. You may well have reached a professional plateau. All that energy and drive to get there and then . . . what? Perhaps your work is just as demanding as it ever was but these days you spend the same amount of hours in the office just in order to stand still and safeguard your position. Your working life is no longer about the exhilaration of climbing but about clinging on for dear life – and job satisfaction is as distant a memory as wearing a suit on Fridays. This is the time in your life when past decisions and patterns of behaviour seem to be gaining on you. You may have been putting sticking plasters over problems in your career, your emotional life or your physical health, but sooner or later these problems will catch up with you. **Now is the time to look at the issues lurking beneath the Bandaids**.

But there is a straw to grasp at. There are plenty of people who have retained high levels of energy into their eighties or even nineties, have a fantastic quality of life and haven't succumbed to illness. Getting old does not have to be all bad – there are huge pluses, even if they aren't always obvious. In order to appreciate them you may have to take a big step back and re-evaluate what you really expect out of life. The definition of 'success', for example, which seemed so clear-cut to you when you were 20 and knew exactly what you were aiming for in your chosen profession or in your relationships, may no longer be valid. What makes us feel as though we are making a success of our lives is different at 20, 30, 40 and beyond. In our first decade in the working world, success is quite measurable – to pass professional exams, to become a partner or head of department, or to achieve some other form of accolade (for me it was a gold medal at the Olympics). Whatever it was, and whether or not we achieved it, as we get older the texture of success becomes infinitely more complex. **Success is as personal as your own fingerprint** – and it is you, not other people, who should be defining your criteria for success. It's no longer about whether your house is on the right side of the street with the right kind of car parked outside. Who envies a three times married self-made multi-millionaire who has more homes than he has friends, more cars than children who speak to him and no focus in his life but how to make the next million? **Making a true success of your life involves finding an overall balance in all the various areas – family, friends, work and, not least, your physical and mental well-being.**

Is it possible to regain the zest you probably took for granted when you were in your twenties and thirties? By helping you to set yourself some goals and encouraging you to evaluate your performance, this book will help you to do just that. It will give you the opportunity to understand many of the physical and psychological changes you are undergoing and to minimise the less welcome trends that have started to manifest.

When I was 20, billions of people round the world watched me carve through the water to win the 100-metre breaststroke in just one minute 3.45 seconds at the 1980 Olympic Games. At that moment, just a quarter (hopefully!) of the way through my life, I had achieved my lifetime ambition. For me, as for many young athletes, reaching this peak so early in life could have presented a real problem. In a curious way, however, the lessons I had learned through the many difficulties I encountered in the years up to that race sustained me way beyond the winning of my Olympic gold. The time leading up to the greatest swim of my life was fraught with physical and psychological obstacles, but in learning how to overcome them, I also discovered some principles of self-motivation and self-confidence that have stood me and many people I have helped in very good stead. My swimming experiences became a microcosm of life and gave me a template for future success.

Some of the biggest obstacles I have faced in life hit me quite early on. My schooldays at Windlesham House, an excellent preparatory boarding school in Sussex, should have been the happiest days of my life; however, they were probably my most miserable. I remember sitting in my English class, aged eight. The master, a thin man with steel-rimmed glasses and cold, unsympathetic eyes looked at me. 'Goodhew II, can you read please?' This was the first time I had been asked to read aloud at my new school and I knew I wasn't any good at it. As I got to my feet I felt myself go cold with fear. All my classmates' eyes were on me and I looked down at the page of hieroglyphics in horror. I managed to decipher the first word on the page but all the rest were a jumble – it was as though a knife was being thrust into the heart of my self-confidence. It wasn't until I was 14 years old that I found out the problem was dyslexia; until then I endured the humiliation of being the class dunce.

As though being labelled stupid wasn't enough, injury was soon to be added to insult. At the age of ten, a fall from a tree (part of an assault course in the school grounds) resulted in the complete and mysterious loss of all my hair within the period of a few months and by the age of 11 I was completely bald. When it was set up there had been much excitement about the assault course, and the school was buzzing with stories about how to survive it. We were put in pairs and as the whistle went I sprinted to the plank of wood which, with another, was secured to two columns to form a narrow bridge. A short way on was the 'big dipper'. Picturing myself as Johnny Weissmuller in *Tarzan* (though without the courage to give the Tarzan cry), I grabbed a rope as far away from me as possible and with hardly a moment's hesitation launched myself into midair. My hands caught hold of the rope and my body started to swing, but at such a young age my wrists weren't strong enough to take that kind of strain. They released automatically and I tumbled through the air towards the ground. It all happened in slow motion. I tried to twist myself into a position where I would land on my feet but instead landed on all fours. My arms couldn't stop my head from crashing into the root of the tree and I hit the sensitive spot under the nose as well as my lip. My front teeth felt as if they had been pushed right back into my mouth, and though I carefully pushed them back into place they were loose for a few days. The next morning my bruised, purple lip had swollen and protruded past my nose. I looked just like the missing link.

The swelling and bruising went down fairly quickly, however, and the whole incident was forgotten within a month; little did I know at the time, however, that the consequences of the fall had by no means come to an end. The first sign I received that all was not well was about a month later. The school had recently broken up and I was at home brushing my hair when I noticed a bare patch on my head. My mother found two more bald patches the size of 10p pieces. This worried her, although at the time I couldn't understand why. It was only later on in life that I began to appreciate that people like normality and a bald-headed 11-year-old is not normal. Hospital tests were organised and I was jabbed, poked, prodded and told that I couldn't do much about it except rub on some cream. The specialist thought it might be caused by shock but what, I wondered, had shock got to do with a few bald patches on my head? The weeks turned into months and, apart from the fact that matron was asked to ensure that I got my daily gunging, things soon got back to normal.

A few months on, however, things livened up when my hair began to fall out in handfuls. Just a week after this started to happen, we had a wrestling lesson and as it was sunny we carried the mats down to one of the lawns near the grass tennis court. In the struggle with my opponent my hair began to rub off all over him and the mat. The master, Mr Roberts, stopped the fight and sent me up to see matron. As I walked up the hill I glanced back. The green mat shone with my golden blond hair. By the next morning there was just a fringe around my head crowning my bright, white bald dome. I looked like a monk. For a while I quite enjoyed the stir I caused, but when I saw the look on the face of the headmaster, Mr Charles, my feelings began to change. It suddenly dawned on me that what had happened was actually very strange and that if I caused Mr Charles to react in this manner then I must look extremely peculiar. I felt a huge fear rising in me, as I knew from my experiences with dyslexia what it felt like to be the odd one out. This was much worse. At least my dyslexia wasn't on display to everybody.

Soon I began to crave the security of home. I woke up the following morning knowing that I was going home on Saturday for what we called a 'leave out'. It meant that we could spend Saturday night at home – we were only allowed two of them every term, and this was one I really needed. With my mousey fringe and shining bald head I felt alone and picked on at school. Even my good friends avoided me – they didn't know what to say.

After activities that afternoon, I was summoned to Mr Charles's office. This always worried me. What had I done wrong? I knocked on his study door and he called me in. As I walked into his oak-panelled study, he walked round to the front of his desk, took a deep breath and told me that my parents had had to cancel my leave out. I felt cold with shock. Slowly the sheer desperation of what had happened started to take effect. The last door of escape from this new reality had been closed. The scream started from my belly and moved into my lungs before it broke physically, tears flowing down my cheeks as my arms thrashed wildly about. Mr Charles calmly took the punches until I exhausted myself. I am not sure to this day why that leave out was cancelled, but looking back I am convinced that a better decision could not have been made (although I have often wondered how Mr Charles broke the news to my mother). As a result I was forced to come to terms with what had happened. It also gave the school a chance to get used to me. I have no doubt that it would have been nearly impossible to take me back to school once I had gone home. So that's the story of how I came to be labelled stupid and bald.

There are many theories on self-motivation, one of which says you should start by making an inventory of your strengths and weaknesses and then set your goals. Unfortunately, when I could really have done with the wisdom of this theory, I was too young to understand it. As a child, my weaknesses in the classroom were painfully obvious and I was struggling to find a strength. I knew I wasn't stupid, yet my school marks said otherwise. As a result, whenever something positive came into my life, I couldn't help noticing it. Swimming was one of the positives, thrown to me like a lifebelt in a storm.

In spite of the trauma of going bald and my poor performance in the classroom, my childhood was in many ways as perfect as anyone might wish for. I had a wealthy and successful father who would drop me off at school in his Bentley, a beautiful and devoted mother and four brothers, and we would spend holidays splashing about in our pool at home in Sussex or at one of our other houses in Alderney or Corfu. That idyll, however, was prematurely shattered by the sudden and totally unexpected death of my father at the age of 57. Overnight, everything changed. Within months, my mother announced to me that she could no longer afford the school fees for Millfield, the exclusive public school, where I had been sent at at the age of 13 to develop my only real strength. The new focus for my energy became to find a way to continue to develop my career as a swimmer.

Rather than being deflected from my ambition, I learned to view any obstacles in my life as springboards to help me move forwards and reach my goals. The need to sustain self-motivation and self-confidence apply as much now as they did in the swimming pool and, in much the same way, many of the principles of physical and mental training are as relevant to the lawyer, the computer programmer or the teacher as they are to the athlete. During my years as a championship swimmer, I learned some tough lessons about the nature of success through both winning and, of course, losing.

You're probably thinking that ordinary life isn't like competitive sport, but you're wrong. **Like all of us, athletes have limited physical resources, and if they are taxed too far, physical exhaustion and plummeting performance will result. The same criteria can be applied to your life whether you are training for the Olympics, studying for accountancy exams or trying to get a new business off the ground.** The questions are the same: where are the margins? Where are the diminishing returns? What type of training will give the best results? What time-scale are you working to? What in the end are you trying to achieve? A programme of diet and exercise combined with a healthy balance of time spent working and time spent on leisure pursuits with family and friends is essential for a sense of well-being whether you are an Olympic athlete or an accountant. Don't worry, I won't be asking you to swim 5,000 metres a day before hitting the commuter train – much smaller adjustments to your routine can make a massive difference to your life. **Think of change in your life like this: a half degree alteration to its course can make a supertanker swing away from a rock on the horizon, or even take it to a different country**. It's a radical thought that a small change can make such a big impact.

We all know men who have lost not just their hair but also their enthusiasm for life, for whom climbing the stairs is an effort and messing about with the kids has become a chore. This book aims to help you find a new spark in your working life, your family life and your social life. It will possibly even increase your life span, and it will certainly improve the quality of your life and give you a greater sense of control. It will tell you how to find the resolve you need to take up this challenge, how to get both your body and your mind in shape, and how to make sure that when things get tough in the office or in your home life you can still get back up there. It will show you how to ensure there is balance in your life, how to train yourself to win and how to build and maintain confidence.

Instead of the insidious sequence of events we described earlier, you could soon be on the ladder of positive improvements which looks like this:

- You resolve to take positive action
- So you start by making some changes in your routine
- So you make some adjustments to your diet
- So you have time and energy for exercise
- So you look and feel better
- So you boost your self-esteem
- So your confidence increases
- So you take charge of changes in your professional and private life
- So you swim

Whether you bought this book for yourself or were given it by a partner, friend or colleague, you might still be in denial at this stage, asking what all this has got to do with you. You are probably slightly dreading any effort that is going to be required on your part. But don't worry, I won't be asking for the impossible. Performing 100 press-ups before a breakfast of freshly squeezed lemon juice and a cup of infused ginger isn't one of the recommendations. The advice in this book is practical, realistic and, above all, achievable. **You are not alone. You are like all people with problems and challenges – the individual context is specific to you but the impact and solutions are very similar**.

At the end of each chapter of *Fix Your Life Now!* there will be a series of action points. These will help you review the messages of the chapter and encourage you to take practical steps towards the changes you need to make. Keep looking back over the action points from previous chapters as you read through the book.

Action

- Find yourself an unused and unlined pad in landscape format.
- Imagine your life as a swimming pool divided into lanes.

Sounds crazy? **The mind is like a parachute – it only works when it's open.** By reading this book and putting our recommendations into practice, you'll find new energy and motivation in your life. It's guaranteed.

CHAPTER 1

TAKING THE PLUNGE –

Step One:
Assess your past, present and future

Think of resolve as a push from the past that meets a pull from the future. It's the incentive which gets you to swim from one end of the pool (away from troubled waters) to the far end (where it's calm). In day-to-day life, it's the driving force which, at one extreme, gets us out of bed in the morning and, at the other, drives us to achieve substantial goals in life. If we don't have aims of some kind we will never achieve much, and if we don't have resolve – or motivation – we'll never get near the starting block let alone off it.

Apathy is most people's worst enemy, and it can strike young. There's nothing more wasteful than just treading water. I looked into this in some detail about ten years ago when I was approached by John Beckwith, a wealthy property developer, who was concerned by the alarming rise in juvenile delinquency. He was willing to invest £1 million of his own money on an initiative which was to become the Youth Sport Trust, the objective of which was to divert children from anti-social behaviour. As any sensible businessman would, he wanted proof that involvement in sport could prevent delinquency before he would part with his money. In addition it was going to take hard evidence for the government to match his investment and thereby ensure long-term support for the project. I worked to provide this evidence with a strategist, Brian Scanlon, who concluded that the majority of young people were afflicted by what he described as 'a habit of aimlessness'. This 'habit' doesn't always leave us, however, and quite often we take it with us into later life. The easy solution to aimlessness is to 'take aim' – to give yourself some goals and then target them.

Someone I met recently had done just that. He was a very successful Danish businessman. He told me how he had once recognised the bartender as he was coming into the Concorde arrivals lounge. 'How are you doing?' asked the bartender, although the answer was fairly obvious. 'Very well,' replied my friend. He went on to confess to the bartender that his motivation to succeed had come almost entirely from the fact that he had been to a smart school where, because his father was a teacher, he had never felt fully accepted. This one thing had driven him to prove himself and had influenced him in every area of his life.

How did I discover my resolve?

My own resolve to make something out of my life was formed when I was still at school. The misery of being dyslexic meant that when I discovered a talent for swimming, I grabbed it with both hands. I clearly remember my first swimming lesson at prep school. I pushed off the wall in the way we'd been told. As my elbows came together, I found my heels had naturally lifted up into the kicking position and I could feel the water against the inside of my feet. As I pushed back against it, my body surged forward through the water. With each stroke I got stronger and more confident and I felt the thrill of doing something properly – until that moment I had not found anything that I could begin to describe myself as good at. Since I was spending most of my time trying to be good at school work (and failing dismally) swimming became a welcome escape from the misery of the classroom.

Everyone has talents, even if they are hard to find. But one thing is sure. If you don't look for them, you won't find them. On many occasions I nearly threw my talents for swimming away, but because of my dyslexia and baldness I never allowed them to drift entirely. One day, as a teenager, in a fit of self-pity and rebelliousness, I stormed into my mother's bedroom. She was brushing her hair and looked up at me. I announced that I was giving up swimming. She paused before resuming her hairbrushing: 'Do whatever you think is best for you,' she said. This completely took the wind out of my sails. I knew in an instant what the 'best' for me was.

I was certain that I would look back some time, perhaps when I was 65, and think, 'What have I done with my life?' I knew that 'I might have' was not the same as 'I have'. I must have heard many adults talking about what they might have been good at, but the stories about the fish that got away didn't seem quite the same as the stories about the fish that was caught and the tasty meal that followed. It struck me that if you were given a talent then it was sacrilege to waste it, and I started to assess where I was with my swimming goals. I had a mental picture of a huge vertical pipe with me hanging on to an iron rung of a ladder inside. Below me the pipe descended into darkness. I looked up and there, somewhere above, I could see a tiny chink of light. I knew that the options were to carry on climbing towards the light and the fulfilment of my goals or to let go and lose all that I had achieved so far. I imagined free-falling down the tube and felt a great sense of waste.

Surely it was better to continue – but how much further could it be?

If I had realised at the time how many more rungs of that ladder I had to climb before reaching Olympic glory, I think I would have had a really tortuous decision to make. It seems to me that there are no right or wrong decisions per se, but only good or bad ones. **A bad decision is when you know what to do but don't do it**. So often we know what to do, and yet find reasons why we shouldn't. I was lucky. I knew what I should do. I went back to swimming. Even at that stage the Olympic spirit had captured my imagination and created a dream which was to drive me on. Years later I stood behind the starting block at the Olympic Games in Moscow, looking down towards the end of the pool. This pool had governed all my decisions for four years. The surface of the water glistened below the intense lighting. My lane, one of eight, was two-and-a-half metres wide, the narrow black strip on the bottom of the pool stretching towards the other end exactly 50 metres away. The lane ropes separating each of the eight swimmers' lanes were 12 centimetres in diameter and were specially designed to dissipate waves so that each swimmer had still water to swim in. I had dreamt of that moment for years, and during the ten months leading up to the Games had been through what seemed like hell to get there, including leaving my family and my country. My past had created a dream that was about to be fulfilled; the push from the past was about to meet the pull from the future.

As well as my difficulties at school and the recognition that we should never waste our talents, death played a fairly significant part in forming my own attitude to life and what I was going to do with it. Two of my friends died while I was at school, one when he was eight. He had shown me his scar from an operation, and (even now the memory of it makes me cringe) I told him I thought he might die. He did, just two weeks later. The other fell to his death from a window. Both these events, together with my father's unexpected death when I was just 16, strengthened my resolve to do something worthwhile in my life.

This backdrop to the first 16 years of my life wasn't exactly full of good fortune, but I regard myself as extremely lucky, largely because the combination of these events has always provided me with the motivation to get out of bed in the morning and 'get on with it'. I felt this push when I was a child and still do today. Even if you have to look harder in your own life for situations that give you a sense of purpose, they are there, and you need to recognise them and make use of them to propel yourself forwards. **Use your past to kick yourself out of the habit of aimlessness.**

The importance of specific goals

It is an essential part of our make-up to have targets which give our lives shape and meaning. Without them, we stagnate. **Without these 'dream events', we don't experience the highs and lows that create interest in our personal landscapes.**

Whether your aim is as banal as getting out of bed in the morning, as life-changing as setting up your own business or as self-improving as learning a new language, having a clear set of goals can change the way you live your life and the satisfaction you derive from it. As Stephen R. Covey writes in his best-selling book *The 7 Habits of Highly Effective People*, 'Begin with the End in Mind.' When you have goals to work to, you immediately put yourself in the driving seat and are in greater control of what happens to you. Having goals means an end to procrastination and to all those excuses you make to yourself about why you haven't got round to doing something. With clearly defined goals you start to take a pro-active role in getting what you want out of life and stop blaming others – or indeed waiting for them to help you achieve something yourself. This is the antithesis of the 'victim' mentality where you have an overdeveloped sense of vulnerability and prefer to feel that the course of your life is not really in your own control. If you achieve a few goals, you will gain confidence in your ability and will then add some more goals, and so the positive cycle (versus the vicious circle) will go on. There are a few self-help theorists from what I call the 'Post-It Note' school who advise their readers to plaster shaving mirror, bedstead, fridge and front door with little stickers exhorting: 'Go For It', 'Take Charge', 'Don't be a Victim' and so on. I'm not sure many partners or wives I know would tolerate the redecoration of their homes in this way, and besides, it's not very British! **Remind yourself persistently (it doesn't have to be out loud) of the things you have promised to do: 'I will take control', 'I will accept responsibility', 'I will embrace change and make it work for me'.** You can look yourself in the eye each morning while you are shaving and say all these' things – even without a yellow sticker to remind you.

When you have a goal, the stages of working towards it (taking aim, working to achieve it, perhaps making sacrifices, and anticipating the outcome) can all provide satisfaction. When working towards my goals, particularly in swimming, I have learned to love detail. Until I was about 20, I found training unbearably dull, but once I had begun to observe and enjoy the different angles of approach, a real appreciation and excitement were added to the drudgery of preparing for competition. I absorbed the minutest of details in swimming just a few lengths:

- feeling the sensation of the water on my skin and how it gripped the surface of my body
- concentrating on streamlining my body through the water
- using the tension in it positively
- combatting pain
- monitoring my times and counting the precise number of strokes in a length

It's often said that the devil is in the detail – though a truer saying is that God is in the detail. Mies van der Rohe, the German architect, put it that way, recognising that there is beauty to be found simply in the detail of form and shape. I focused on finding interest in every aspect of my training and in doing so discovered new levels of pleasure and reward.

Knowing your goals gives you something to aim for and puts you firmly in control. **If you don't know what your dream is, how can you experience the pleasure of having it come true?** It is worth setting both short- and long-term goals: short-term goals give immense satisfaction by being achievable in the near future and spur you on to reach the others. They should be immediately realisable targets, such as renewing contact with someone you have lost touch with, visiting a place you have always wanted to see, getting up ten minutes early to walk to the station rather than going by car. Even such easily reachable targets will give you a feeling of forward momentum, a rhythmic stroke that pulls you closer and closer to your dream event. **Don't procrastinate with these short-term goals, make a start on them now.**

Understanding where you are at present

One very useful and revealing way to look at where you are at present – and to help you see where to go in future – is to pick up a pencil and draw. Haven't done any drawing since primary school? Don't worry if you're no Leonardo, you don't need to be. The fact is that by using the creative side of your brain you are bound to bring something to the fore that will not emerge using words.

Start by drawing an image of how you picture your life today. I've used this technique a great deal with business people – a group who so often neglect their creative side – and many have commented that it was an extremely clarifying experience. As well as drawing where you are today, you can also use this same tool to visualise what you want in your future. Keep the pictures you draw and revisit them from time to time to see whether and how your perspective changes – and keep drawing. If there is someone you trust, do the exercise together and explore your explanations of the results. Remember, a picture can be worth a thousand words.

Swim in new waters

Longer-term plans could include learning a new skill, taking some professional exams or giving up smoking. They can have quantifiable or precisely measurable ends (to get a new job or lose four kilograms in weight, for example), or they might be considerably more abstract (to feel more generally contented, or to be more patient with the kids).

Your goals should all be ones which you can write down in a list, and you should commit yourself to them – putting them on paper is an important first step towards making them happen. Once they are there, in black and white, you can't forget them or pretend they don't exist. You can always revisit the list and add to it – or even reconsider the goals if your priorities change. The following framework will help you fathom out what really matters to you and will help you define your goals:

SEE – new places, new people, new views, new perspectives, new detail

HEAR – listen and explore more

FEEL – give your instincts an airing

TASTE – enjoy the taste of life – savour what's good and bin the bad

CREATE – think about what you will leave behind you

Take some time right this moment to think about these 'senses'. Make lists – practical or abstract, it doesn't matter at this stage – of ideas and actions that spring to mind under these headings. Using these tools, set goals in the following areas: the workplace, your home, your family, your friends and what I would loosely describe as your personal development. If you have been doing the same things, in the same way, in the same place with the same people for 20 years, it is likely that you have neglected your personal development. Have you a creative spark? Or are you stagnating? **To learn and develop you need to swim in new waters.**

Being prepared to change how you live – and how you are

Underscoring the idea of working towards a goal is the notion of change. In order to achieve the goals you set for yourself, action and effort are required – and invariably the willingness to alter your own attitudes in some way. There will always be a little voice inside saying, 'Don't bother, it's far too much effort', 'It's not the right time so why not wait a while', 'It's inconvenient', 'Don't try, you might fail'. That voice is strident and sometimes deafening, and it will be easier to listen to it than to get on with trying to achieve your aims. You have to keep reminding yourself that you are in control of your life and that if you have made a decision to achieve a certain goal, then you can and will rise to the challenge. Remember, the main obstacle will usually be yourself.

Some of your goals might involve making big changes in your life. Others might involve more subtle changes and yet have a very significant effect on your life. Say, for example, you decide to leave the car at home and take a very brisk 20-minute walk to the station. It sounds pretty unexciting as a goal, but the possible benefits are:

- no stress from sitting in a traffic jam
- no angst trying to find somewhere to park
- 40 minutes a day of healthy exercise – that's three hours and 20 minutes a week
- time and space to think about the day
- money saved on fuel and car-parking
- a contribution to the environment

The spin-off benefits from a simple change such as this aren't hard to quantify. A friend of mine who was in a rut with his job recently resolved to make a small change in his life which has made a huge impact on the overall picture. He had been arriving at the office each morning at 7.30 a.m. and working a good 11-hour day. He was getting home at 8.30 p.m. exhausted and fit for nothing but bed. He took my advice to carry on leaving for work at 7.30 a.m. (he was naturally an early riser) but to spend an hour in the gym three mornings a week before going to the office. He now arrives in the office at 8.30 a.m. having done an hour's work-out and feeling energised and ready to face the day. He usually leaves work much earlier than he used to, having achieved more in a shorter time than before he started this new regime. His boss has noticed his increased productivity, his staff appreciate his improved mood, his wife is delighted with the fitter, happier model and his kids are thrilled to see him home in time for their bed-time stories. **Less is more – and we all deserve more, don't we?**

The challenge

Goals in areas other than your career may not really have seemed to matter when you were in your twenties. There was the happy delusion that life would simply go on forever and there would always be time to make up your mind about what you wanted to get out of it and to go after those things. Once you find yourself in the region of 40, however, you have to face up to the fact that you are now probably somewhere around the half-way mark.

Don't despair. What better time to address all those dissatisfactions with your life and your body than now. **Think of it as half-time – analyse your performance in the first half and plan the new strategy for the second half of your life:**

- So it's half-time
- So you review the first half
- So you see where the ruts are in your life
- So you dream of new possibilities
- So you set some goals
- So you decide on the action you should take
- So you rise out of the apathy you were in
- So the stagnant water starts to move

What is there that you need more of? Or less of? Think of the time-scale and make some plans. It's important to square any major changes with those closest to you and take them along with you in your decision-making so that they are supportive and understand why you have decided to spend three hours a week at the gym, to learn to fly or to change career. After all, any of these changes will have an impact on those around you, and you need to persuade them that what is good for you is good for them too, not an inconvenience, irritation or loss. **One thing we fear about change is that we will lose something.** So concentrate on the potential gains as you strike out towards the far end of your pool.

In a competition swimming pool, the end of each lane is marked with a cross, pulling you inexorably towards your goal. In addition to the crosses that keep you heading in a straight line, there are blue and white lane ropes which help give you a sense of moving forwards as you pass each metre length. Think of the lanes as the different areas of your life (work, family, partner, friendships, self-development, etc.) and aim for the crosses, your goal for each area.

Action

- List your 'pushes from the past'.
- List your main achievements which have been, or still are, your 'pulls to the future'.

	YOUR SWIMMING POOL			
	STEP 1	STEP 2	STEP 3	GOAL
	STEP 1	STEP 2	STEP 3	GOAL
YOUR SWIMMING LANES	STEP 1	STEP 2	STEP 3	GOAL
	STEP 1	STEP 2	STEP 3	GOAL
	STEP 1	STEP 2	STEP 3	GOAL
	STEP 1	STEP 2	STEP 3	GOAL
	STEP 1	STEP 2	STEP 3	GOAL

YOUR FINISHING POINTS

- Turn to a blank double-page spread in your pad and divide it into rows across both pages, so it looks like a swimming pool.
- At the right-hand end of each lane, write down one of your major goals. These should be in all the areas of your life: work, home, family, relationship with partner, friends, recreation, fitness, etc.
- From left to right, write down the steps you need to take in order to reach your main goals. These will act as your stepping stones or hand-holds, and reaching them will give you the short-term encouragement you need to keep swimming and sustaining a strong sense of forward momentum.
- Monitor your major goals on a regular basis to assess how far you have come.
- Add new goals.
- Commit yourself to celebrating the successful achievement of your goals and write down how you will do this in the appropriate swimming lanes.
- Keep souvenirs of your successes close to hand – they'll be a great encouragement when you're feeling a failure.

CHAPTER 2

GETTING INTO THE SWIM –

Step Two: Find your healthy level of stress

Although some of the key events in our lives are outside our control, mostly we should aim to be holding the reins. Ask yourself, **if you aren't in the driving seat of your life by the time you are 40, when will you be?** If you aren't in control, then who is? You are too old still to be wearing L-plates. Between the inevitable cornerstones of birth and death (and taxes), you should be in charge of your own destiny even if, at times, you feel as though you're being swept along with the tide and out to sea.

I meet plenty of people who remind me of pyromaniacs, pouring petrol on a fire that's already raging. What they fail to notice is that they are the ones who are burning — burning out quite literally. I recently worked with a number of executives in a large corporation; one in 20 was unable even to make the course, and 25 per cent of those who did were on their way to burn-out either physically or psychologically before retirement. And, incidentally, the retirement age was 55! I find that shocking, horrifying, but, sadly, all too typical. On the other hand, I do meet people who are completely in control of their own destiny — because they have made the decision to be. One such person is a client of mine, a partner in a big multi-national firm, who realised that he could only feel in control if he cast off the routine of a daily commute and a rigid 9 a.m. to 7 p.m. working day. He started to work at home for two days a week, at hours that suited him, making all the necessary allowances for the fact that he has to make space for his colleagues when they need him. The evidence of this new-found freedom is the fact that, in many months, he hasn't once had to buy a weekly season ticket. The variety he enjoys in his schedule means that he no longer feels as though he is living in a rut. He defined what 'control' meant in his own life, worked out how to achieve it, informed others and made it happen. It is well worth contemplating your current lifestyle to see whether there are such significant improvements you could make yourself.

At this stage of reading this book, identify where you are on the 'shock curve' illustrated opposite. **Are you in denial? Are you at the blame stage? Or are you open to learning and developing?**

The process of change – and your reaction

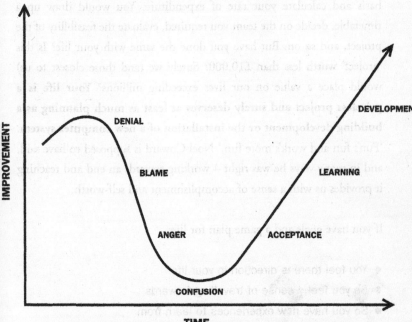

This diagram illustrates the common reaction to change. It shows the stages people go through when confronted by some home truths which demand action or response on their part.

The clearly defined set of goals described in the last chapter is an essential starting point for giving ourselves a sense of control over what happens to us. Achieving them will encourage us to keep hold of the controls. If you haven't yet set your goals, spend some time comparing how you run your own life with how you organise things at work. Imagine a task where you have to manage a project with a fixed budget and an approximate time-scale. The budget might be anywhere between £10,000 and £100,000, or may even run into millions. You would carefully plan a strategy, detail how the project would be managed, decide what had to be achieved during each phase, work out your expectations on a monthly basis and calculate your rate of expenditure. You would draw up a timetable, decide on the team you required, evaluate the feasibility of the project, and so on. But have you done the same with your life? Is this 'project' worth less than £10,000? Surely we (and those closest to us) would place a value on our lives exceeding millions? **Your life is a priceless project and surely deserves at least as much planning as a building development or the installation of a new computer system**. 'Fun's fun and work's more fun,' Noel Coward is supposed to have said, and in many ways he was right – working towards an end and reaching it provides us with a sense of accomplishment and self-worth.

If you have goals and a game plan for life:

- You feel there is direction in your life
- So you feel a sense of travelling forwards
- So you have new experiences to learn from
- So you feel you are developing and expanding as a person
- So you get a sense of achievement
- So you look for new interests and explore new openings
- So you set yourself new goals

The imperative goal is to get yourself into peak physical and mental condition. This will be a springboard for higher achievement in all your other goals and will help in defending you against the unforeseen – whether it's the kids failing their exams, your job being at risk after a take-over, or the illness of someone close to you. When you have some of the handholds in place, if any of these things happen you are in a much better position to deal with them, and you won't feel that you have entirely lost control. **Ask yourself whether the tasks you are engaged in actually fit your goals**. Check that you aren't spending too much time on things that make no contribution to your longer-term plans and what you feel is important in your life.

What can make us feel out of our depth?

Let's look at some of the issues that can make us feel out of control and unable to cope, and consider the difference between those where we can take action and those where we simply have to rely on our inner strength.

SITUATIONS WE CAN'T CONTROL
Illness and injury

Death, of course, is the ultimate loss of control, and sooner or later it will happen – even if books like this help you take longer to get there. Illness and injury will also happen to you from time to time – they are not entirely unavoidable. There is much you can do, however, to minimise the inevitable – by taking safety measures to avoid injury and as many health precautions as you can without becoming obsessive!

Be vigilant about any changes in your own body and make sure you have regular medical check-ups – if your company offers you an annual health and fitness screening, make sure you book in. As well as checking such essentials as your blood pressure, cholesterol levels, weight, prostate etc. they are likely to offer you some general health advice (taking your overall level of fitness into account). Men are notoriously apathetic about their health and visit their GP much less frequently than women – even though the difference between making an appointment and ignoring tell-tale signs of illness may be one of life and death. Here's a cautionary tale of two men I met last year. One of them is a managing director of a multi-national company who went for a health check and was informed that he had a major heart problem. Preparations were rapidly made for life-saving surgery. He went into immediate denial and claimed that he absolutely had to attend an important meeting in India. Eventually he recognised the magnitude of the situation and consented to the operation, which was successful. The deal in India was not affected. The other chap was the chairman of a local council leisure department; I met him when I was doing an inaugural swim at a pool in his area. He decided to swim with me. Breakfast consisted of bacon rolls, which I avoided, and after the swim he collapsed following a massive heart attack. Although everything was done to keep him alive, he was dead on arrival at the hospital. I heard later that he had been to see a specialist the day before and was booked in for heart-bypass surgery which was to have taken place just two days later. His denial led him to ignore the risk he took by swimming on a full stomach with a serious heart condition. Don't think you're immune from such stupidity. When did you last visit your doctor or have a full physical fitness test?

(For more information see Appendices I–VI.)

Bereavement

Experiencing the death of a close relative or friend can feel like the worst possible loss of control, but it can also create an urgency in your own life. It makes you confront your own mortality and may strengthen your resolve to do something with your own life, thereby making a positive out of what is otherwise an entirely bleak event.

Redundancy

Given that many men are defined by their work, losing a job is a major crisis. As well as income you may lose status, the feeling of having a particular place to go to and particular tasks to achieve each day, and the vital sense of having a role in life. All of this can be felt as keenly as bereavement. If you are made redundant, this anecdote might encourage you:

A patient visits his psychologist. 'I'm getting married,' he says. The psychologist insists on opening a bottle of wine. 'Let me commiserate with you over all the opportunities you've lost,' he says. His next patient brings the news that he has lost his job. 'Let's celebrate all the new opportunities now open to you,' he urges.

The psychologist is clearly not a man who needs an excuse for a drink, but in many ways his positive attitude with his second patient is just right.

The birth of a child

If you are a father, you were undoubtedly delighted when your children were born. In all likelihood they were planned and you felt the whole business was under your control. But even so, the birth of children turns your lifestyle on its head, disrupts your sleeping patterns, and gives your relationship with your partner an entirely new dimension. It's easy to lose your sense of humour and perspective on the situation, especially when you're suffering from sleep deprivation.

Children growing up

If we had known in advance about all the potential problems to be encountered as our children grow up, some of us might have thought twice about parenthood. Learning and behavioural difficulties, illness or simply the agony of their adolescence can create change in our lives almost weekly. The time eventually comes for them to go off to pursue further education or leave home entirely – and this, of course, brings as major a change as the day they were born.

There is little we can do to avoid these life changes. What we can do, however, is prepare ourselves by becoming strong enough to deal with them. Then we will not be knocked completely off course when they happen. Some of them, in fact, can have a silver lining and provide new opportunities. I was taking a shower at my sports club a couple of years ago when someone I worked out with began to vent his frustration about his job as an executive in an advertising agency. His seniority and success were reflected by the car he drove – a Ferrari – but he had a burning desire to get out of advertising into fashion and retail. I warned him it was risky, that retail, like catering and building, have the highest level of business failure, but I said that if he felt it was something he must do then he should do it all the same, otherwise he would always regret it. As it turned out, he was under-capitalised and his new business failed. At the same time he found out that his wife was having an affair. He caught her *in flagrante* in his own house. At this point in his life he felt completely out of control in every area. Now, however, he has a leading position in the motor racing world, he lives a few miles from his office, in the centre of the village where he was born, and he is contemplating marriage once again. His clouds certainly turned out to have a silver lining, though he went through a few thunderstorms before he discovered it.

SITUATIONS WE CAN CONTROL

There are other areas of anxiety where you can take steps to equip yourself with the necessary skills. Rather than moaning and whingeing about change, you can be the one taking steps to overcome the obstacles and meet the challenges. We're all inclined to say 'I don't have time to . . .', but time spent now is time saved later on (particularly with health issues).

Worries about illness

If you are concerned about a possible health problem, take action by consulting your GP and putting yourself on the fitness trail.

Stress at work

A heavy workload, difficult colleagues, a new boss – numerous different aspects of your working life can easily get on top of you. You need to ensure that you have techniques to counteract the effects of such pressures – and however bad things seem to be remember that there are always options; you have control over these.

Starting a new job

A new job may entail increased responsibility, and you will need to ensure that your family and friends understand the new demands on you.

New technology

New technology can be bewildering, time-consuming and exasperating. The only way to resolve this is by making sure you are completely up to date with the training on offer and refusing to bury your head in the sand. Don't get computer-rage – computers are only machines that are meant to make your life easier. However, they only do so if you make time to understand how to operate them.

Pressure of relationships

As parent, child or spouse we are often trying to please or perform – and we might experience intense feelings of demoralisation if we seem to be failing. As long as you are not short-changing your friends and family by not giving them enough time or commitment they will probably not be too judgemental. If these relationships are in good order, your family should love you unconditionally (and vice-versa!).

Moving house

When you move house your day-to-day routine is suddenly no longer the same: friends and neighbours you had grown accustomed to aren't there to support you, and as for the list of DIY tasks . . . Give yourself time to settle into your new environment and get to know your neighbours – and don't feel that you must have your new home looking perfect by the end of your first week in it.

Minor stresses

Minor stresses that can escalate into major causes of stress are events such as getting stuck in traffic, losing keys and missing deadlines. Many of these can be resolved by improved organisation and management of your time and space.

Turning difficulties into opportunities

Try and put yourself in control of the situation and set out to eliminate the problems systematically. **Try to see the difficulties as challenges, the struggles as potential adventures and the obstacles as opportunities to test yourself, rather than situations which will completely overwhelm you.** It is all a question of attitude. The process of moving yourself into a position of control can be a painful one and, let's not pretend otherwise, it can take a great deal of effort.

The pain involved in taking control is well illustrated by the stages of physical training that an athlete has to go through to get ready for competition. During my competitive swimming days, the only way I could hope to be in control of my situation as I stepped onto the starting block was by leaving nothing to chance in the weeks and months leading up to that moment. I remember that the vacation training before the Moscow Olympics in 1980 was particularly gruelling. The session started at 4.30 a.m. so we were up every morning at 4.05 a.m. We started with 45 minutes of weight training, followed by a one-and-a-half-mile run. We would then move on to a circuit with 11 stations, each morning doing five of them, picking up where we had finished the previous day. The first morning I had to swim 1500 metres butterfly with a part inflated car inner tube around my waist. After that it was the gaff rigs. Around my waist I buckled a belt with a rope attached to it that extended up and around a pulley system attached to the gaff rig. At the end of the rope was a shopping basket with lead weights in it. We had to keep the basket out of the water, and it only took a quick glance by the coach to tell whether or not we had enough weight in the basket.

Once the coach had found the correct weight, your stroke developed a drowning quality. Then it was out of the water to the crutches (which were too short for us) and tied up legs. Up and down the hill we went, 12 times. Our shoulder muscles were already tired and the crutches dug into our ribs. The next exercise was similar to a child's wheelbarrow game. We walked on our hands for three-quarters of a mile dragging our feet behind us on a small dolly cart. For the finale we had to climb up and down a rope from ceiling to floor 20 times. We were still in our swimsuits and our skin was still soft from being submerged in water for 40 minutes. If we used our legs, the skin was stripped from our ankles and feet, so we had to use our arms. That evening we swam 7,500 metres. It sounds masochistic. Perhaps it was. But the pain I suffered would have been less than the pain of winning an Olympic silver medal by 0.03 of a second.

This training was about more than developing specific skills. Getting a feel for the water and a sense of my time and place in the race, and developing the flexibility to move more efficiently through the clinging water – these were my aims. Increasing the strength, power and endurance to overcome my adversaries and the tolerance to get through the pain barrier were also on the agenda. This was the preparation I needed in order to be in control, and you will have an equivalent in your own situation.

Identify the source of pressure

If we are under pressure, we need to step back and ask whether we are being pressurised by others or ourselves. If it is the latter we need to decide whether the goalposts should be moved. Quite often deadlines are self-imposed and it is always worth questioning whether you stand to lose more by delaying the completion or by busting a gut to meet an impossible deadline. Quite often, it will only be you who is damaged by choosing the second option. Make sure you aren't setting yourself difficult deadlines just to prove something to yourself, or others. It's worth asking yourself, your client or your boss, 'Do you want a slapdash job – or a job properly done?' If it's the latter and you need more time, then say so. **There are no medals for masochists**. It's OK to attempt to walk on water occasionally, but catastrophic to do it on a regular basis – you'll drown.

It's very poor and irresponsible corporate strategy to have no slack in the company's system – the system will break down, and succession will become a problem if the mid-ranking executives are continually getting burnt out. This is probably quite a typical story: the wife of one of my clients was convinced her husband was having an affair. He was getting in very late at night and disappearing in the morning before she was even awake. The only evidence that he'd been home at all was a dirty shirt in the corner of the bedroom. She confronted him with the accusation, and when he protested that his long hours away from home were genuinely being spent at work, she insisted that he went to his superiors. 'We wondered when you'd come,' they said. 'You've been doing enough work for three people.' They had clearly been taking advantage and found it amusing that it had taken him so long to wake up to his situation. He renegotiated the roles and responsibilities of his job and overnight developed a sense of humour. It was as though his personality had been drowned under his workload.

If the goalposts have been set by someone else and you feel uncomfortable with them, why not query where they have been positioned and get them moved? If you are told that they can't be moved, and the result is an unmanageable level of stress, it is probably a good idea to consider whether you are in the right job. High levels of stress, as well as making your life miserable, can also do you irreparable damage. What is worth more? Your job or your well-being? There is a tendency in many of us for catastrophe thinking. **Rather than letting go of a deadline and negotiating to move the goalposts, we hurtle towards it in a blind panic**. How insecure are you? Will you really lose your job?

Someone who put himself firmly back in the driving seat of his own life was Rod, a partner from a leading global professional services firm who had taken part in the executive survival course I had ran. I caught up with him recently and he described the path his life had taken since then. One of the messages he took away from the course was the importance of shedding some of the adrenalin that built up during a week spent working in a highly stressful environment. He found that by taking regular exercise rather than collapsing on Saturday mornings he gained new energy and enthusiasm for his family. He also learned to partition his diary (we'll talk about that in more detail in Chapter 4), making sure he made space for himself and his hobbies. He got back into his local rugby first team, resumed his shooting career and in the summer spent time scuba diving. He also lost two stone. He was a changed man and for three or four years he was absolutely in control of his life. Things changed, however, when he was promoted from a domestic position in the firm to one of global leadership in one of the practice areas which involved regular and extensive travel to the States, Europe and the Far East. Everything (including his physique) then went pear-shaped. The pattern of travel (Bombay–Calcutta–Seoul and home again in just a few days, for example) meant that he couldn't take any exercise. His diary on these trips would be organised by the local offices whose attitude was: 'This is an important man, every minute of his time must be filled.' In this context he no longer had the protection of his secretary, who would schedule time for going to the gym or having a swim.

As he describes it himself: 'I was literally bouncing from one hotel to another – and there's a limit to the callasthenics you can do in an aircraft toilet.' In the second year of this helter-skelter lifestyle, alarm bells began to ring. He was missing out on seeing his children growing up, his weight was increasing and his fitness levels were plummeting. His levels of stress were none too healthy either. The control he wanted to have over his own life was quite literally being taken away by other people. He had to do something about it, and the simple solution was to 'retire'. At 46 years of age, he has moved to Cornwall with his family and is starting a company of his own – a diving business. He is back at the helm. Back in control and poised quite literally to swim in new waters.

Stress – still with us in the 21st-century

Stress is a hangover from the twentieth century. We should have left it behind, along with bulging filofaxes, 6 a.m. breakfast meetings, power dressing and the yuppy. Sadly, we don't seem entirely able to shake it off. Most of us are apparently addicted to an impossible pace of life, and the phenomenon of stress seems stuck to us like chewing gum on a shoe. Is there a man or woman you know who never refers to it at some point? Who never says 'I'm feeling a bit stressed' or 'I've had a really stressful day'? – even children go round telling each other not to be so 'stressy'. Stress has even taken over from the common cold as the most used excuse to miss work. Maybe it has always existed and we just called it something else – said we were 'under pressure', 'at the end of our tether' or just 'finding it hard to cope'. Stress has always been a possibility, but perhaps the pace at which we live and the amount we expect ourselves to achieve in a day has accelerated to such an extent that it's now virtually institutionalised; **we all get sucked into the fast lane and dragged and buffeted along in each other's slipstream**. If, for example, we are always available at the end of a mobile phone, where are those quiet moments of respite from our clients, boss or colleagues which allowed us to recharge our batteries? Even a laptop computer, useful as it is for working when we are away from the office, means that the time when we might have been sitting on a train gazing out of the window and having a few minutes of quiet reflection, planning or just complete relaxation, is now spent in frenetic activity. Technology can pollute our lives. Even if we can deal with the stress of making it work for us, it can be a rod for our own backs, since it has created the possibility and therefore the demand for speed, instant access and immediacy. The phrase 'It's in the post' will be soon be consigned to the phrase-book graveyard, as outdated and unused as 'My postilion has been struck by lightning'. Such excuses no longer have any validity – everything can be emailed, faxed or posted on the web NOW and if you don't act immediately, those around you will be wanting to know why.

Is it any wonder, then, that we all occasionally feel stressed? Unless we live the solitary life of a hermit in the Outer Hebrides (in fact, there's even a BT call centre there now!), it's likely that the pace of life will sometimes get to us – and sometimes get us down. It's when we can't shake that feeling off and 'stressed' becomes our normal state of being that we should really begin to worry. Being overwhelmed by stress is like sitting at the wheel of a car, the brakes have gone and we are accelerating downhill. We need to be able to get back in control, but before we know what has happened, the steering wheel has come away in our hands. And as well as adversely affecting our attitudes to life and how we feel day-to-day, stress can trigger symptoms that lead to serious physical problems and long-term illness.

Some people are naturally more predisposed to anxiety than others and will be more susceptible to feelings of being unable to cope. Others seem able to deal with whatever life throws at them and remain calm even under apparently impossible pressure. At one extreme are those who suffer panic attacks when they're stuck queuing for a train ticket, at the other are those who seem to sail through life without a care in the world. **Wherever you fall on the scale, everyone has a point where they start to fall to pieces, either physically, psychologically or both – no one is immune.**

It is worth examining the nature of stress, understanding what happens to our bodies when we are under it and learning to recognise the danger signals. It would be unrealistic to suggest that you can go through life without experiencing any stress, but you should learn to identify the tell-tale signs that warn us that the body is reaching its limit of tolerance. **It's important to know the point at which stress becomes corrosive and begins to do us damage. Action is essential at this point.**

A primitive chain reaction

Our bodily reactions to stress are essentially very primitive, and haven't changed since we were hunter-gatherers. When we are exposed to danger of any kind (a high-pressure situation with work colleagues, for example), the 'fight or flight' response is triggered. When we were more primitive beings this meant that confronted by a predatory wild animal we had a choice to make: either to fight it or to run away. Whichever course of action we took, a chain of spontaneous reactions had already geared up our bodies to respond.

The fight or flight reaction is activated by the sympathetic (or autonomic) nervous system, which is, in effect, preparing us for rapid movement by increasing levels of oxygen in the bloodstream. The specific chain of events is as follows:

- The 'danger' signal is sent deep into the part of the brain known as the hypothalamus . . .
- which alerts the pituitary gland . . .
- which activates the adrenal glands (situated above the kidneys) . . .
- which produce adrenalin and noradrenalin. (We are all familiar with the sensation created by a rush of adrenalin, something that we also feel when we are excited.)

At the same time:

- The liver releases blood sugars to be used by the muscles once action begins.
- The heart pumps harder and breathing becomes regulated, forcing oxygen into the system (required by the muscles to help transform sugar into energy) and causing blood pressure to rise.
- The bladder and bowels evacuate any excess.
- Sweat is produced in order to cool the body down in preparation for the anticipated exertion.
- The tensed muscles release lactic acid into the bloodstream.
- The pupils dilate to improve vision, making us extra alert and sensitive to outside stimuli.
- Non-essential bodily functions such as digestion and salivation shut down. (This is why the mouth goes dry when we are under stress.)

If you are unprepared for these symptoms . . .

All of these sensations were all too familiar in my early days of competitive swimming. Although I wasn't trying to escape a man-eating shark, in some ways I often felt as though I was swimming for my life. I remember very clearly my first race in an Olympic-sized pool when I was 11. My body displayed all the classic symptoms of stress, and because of my inexperience I completely failed to recognise and deal with them. There were huge numbers of spectators and a great deal of noise, and the pool looked terrifyingly long. My throat went completely dry and I was excessively thirsty. I'd need all the energy I could get, or so I told myself, and dug into my tracksuit pocket for another glucose tablet. It was a mistake as the glucose absorbed what little moisture was left in my mouth, leaving me parched and with no time to get a drink. Time seemed to stand still until, at last, it was our turn and all I wanted to do was finish the race and go and quench my thirst. As I swam, the air going into my lungs burnt my dry throat and when I came up for breath I took in some spray which choked me. I gasped for air and in panic breathed in more water. The next time I came up I managed to fill my lungs with air, but it was too late. The damage had already been done. My body had been starved of oxygen and I was suffering from what I now know to be oxygen debt. All the muscles in my body began to ache at the same time and my legs felt as if they were going to explode. I gasped for more air, but I had nothing left and when I finished I had to be helped from the pool. I vowed never to make that mistake again – in front of my parents and literally thousands of spectators I had been dragged out of the pool like a non-swimmer. Eric the Eel would have beaten me that day.

This disastrous race was an illustration of what can happen when you allow stress to build up rather than being aware of it and dealing with it. I should have recognised why I was thirsty, but I simply made it worse by dosing myself with glucose. My breathing was already heavy, but rather than trying to calm myself and control it. I simply gasped in more air. A version of the same sense of panic, breathlessness and inability can overwhelm you when you are under stress in your working or even your family life. The office, hospital, school or wherever you work all present occasions where you will be tested to the limit. It can also be an affliction in family life, where dealing with tricky children or marital breakdown can create a serious amount of stress.

What happens if you have too much stress?

All of the automatic fight or flight reactions were vital in a more primitive environment, but today, in our generally safe, unthreatening world, the physical effort which they prepare us for isn't always required. Even if you are involved in a major boardroom showdown, it is unlikely that you'll resolve the issues by rolling up your sleeves and having a fist fight. Passions may be running very high, but in our civilised times we rarely find solutions through resorting to physical violence (when we do, it makes the headlines). At moments when tempers flare, our adrenalin levels have risen to help us deal with a situation. If the adrenalin is not then burnt up, the effects of its secretion into our system can lead to a range of problems. **Adrenalin doesn't disappear, it lingers in the system.** You may all too easily find yourself caught up in the following vicious circle:

- You're adrenalised
- So you feel threatened
- So another incident is likely to take place
- So you feel on edge
- So you become adrenalised once again

After a week or so of this cycle you can have up to three times your safe level of adrenalin. Some adrenalins have a half-life of around 18 hours, thereby compounding the initial effect every time you are adrenalised. At some point, you will start to rely on adrenalin for what you now perceive as a normal way of life. When you dip, for example, and can't find situations to adrenalise you, you might reach for the coffee pot and a fix of caffeine to re-elevate the system – or perhaps you reach for something much worse. I had a client who was a perfect case-study of over-adrenalisation. He was impossible to deal with. He was erratic, irrational and volatile, and at meetings he would grab a detail irrelevant to the progression of any discussion and go back to it like a baby to its pacifier. His behaviour was a good illustration of the fact that the adrenalin response is a by-product of a survival system that we no longer need, but have not yet evolved away from. In a highly adrenalised situation, the brain can only deal with the 'kill' or 'run' response and my client was demonstrating this by clinging on to a single detail, a stong focus. The simple fact is this: **we were not designed to polish chairs. Our day-to-day situations now are much more complex than the 'fight or flight' ones that used to preoccupy us.** Sometimes the correct responses are *not* those which come naturally to the body and brain – they are the opposite. You don't want to show these symptoms in a meeting do you?

The physical and emotional effects

An excess of adrenalin can lead to an increase in the rate and depth of breathing, which in turn can lead to heart-pounding and tightening of the chest (which could well be interpreted as a danger signal from the heart) and high blood pressure. Similarly, if you are over-aroused for a long period, head-, neck- and backache are likely to result, as is difficulty in sleeping. Digestive disorders such as irritable bowel syndrome can also be triggered by stress. Experiencing any of these problems simply leads to more stress and feelings of being out of control.

Every time the body's fight or flight reaction is set in motion, energy is diverted from the normal bodily functions of digesting, cleansing and rejuvenating. What is the inevitable result of this? That you will age faster. And if your body is subjected to prolonged stress, your pituitary gland, pancreas and liver will be continually pumping out hormones to keep your blood sugar down and will start to suffer from all this wear and tear. If premature ageing isn't enough to make you determined to minimise the stress in your life, then perhaps life-threatening illness such as heart disease and cancer is.

Given the dramatic impact that stress can have on your happiness, your health and the length of your life, isn't it worth making certain that you keep it to a minimum? An entirely stress-free life would probably be very unexciting and sedentary – and, ironically, stressful in its monotony. To minimise stress and feel in control are aims worth having.

For many years I worked with Malcolm Emery, a bright and charismatic physiologist who owned a substantial share in a health screening business. He had thousands of corporate executives coming through his screening centres every year, and this afforded him an extraordinary insight into the result of the unsustainable lifestyles within corporate life. He would often use the pressure-performance curve illustrated below to show his patients what they were subjecting themselves to. Quite simply, beyond a certain point your performance will suffer badly – and perhaps irretrievably.

What happens if you are under too much stress

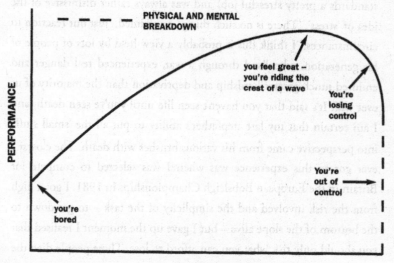

The thrill of surfing on the edge of life is compelling and what many of us seek. All too often, however, we 'over rev' and begin to slip down the slope of declining performance. After one deadline has been met, another takes its place allowing you no time to get back on the crest. In normal circumstances you'll probably survive, but illness, the death of someone close or the eruption of any number of other personal or business problems will tip you over the edge. No one is immune from this, although we all have a different set of triggers and will be affected in different areas – the back, the prostate, the heart, the chest, the emotions, the rational self. Eventually, if you don't allow yourself to recover, you will lose control – and the end result could be a nervous or physical breakdown. Or maybe you will hold on and die shortly after retirement. Unfortunately, it's tragically common.

Is there an alternative to stress?

A view of the world which I very much admire was that held by my stepfather. He was an ace pilot, promoted to Air Vice Marshal, (by most standards a pretty stressful job) and was always rather dismissive of the idea of 'stress'. 'There is no such thing,' he claimed, 'just our reaction to circumstances.' I think this is probably a view held by lots of people of his generation, who lived through a war, experienced real danger and endured much greater hardship and deprivation than the majority of us ever will. It's said that you haven't seen life until you've seen death, and I am certain that my late stepfather's ability to put all the 'small stuff' into perspective came from his various brushes with death. The closest I ever got to this experience was when I was selected to compete for Britain in the European Bobsleigh Championships in 1981. I got a high from the risk involved and the simplicity of the task – to get down to the bottom of the slope alive – but I gave up the moment I realised that you should only risk what you can afford to lose. Three people died the year I competed, and of the team that did a stunt in a James Bond movie (our team had been asked and had refused) one was killed. Taking part was probably the most exhilarating experience I ever had, but possibly the most addictive too. I had come face to face with the pull of adrenalin and seen how you could come to rely on it to feel really alive.

In search perhaps of some missing excitement in life, we in our post-war generation have imposed on ourselves a faster pace of life. We're like athletes doped to the eyeballs, competing with reckless disregard for the future. We think we need to sprint all day long when what we would benefit from much more is an even marathon pace with time to look at the view and enjoy what is around us. **Life is just like swimming – it's very easy – once you relax you float, and little effort is required to sustain a good speed**.

The reactions described above, which make you ready for fight or flight, are reactions to *perceived* threat. We sometimes need to look that threat in the face and ask ourselves whether it is really endangering us at all. Was my stepfather right? Do we just need to react differently? Is this how to gain a greater sense of control?

Get yourself organised

It's amazing how much stress you can cause yourself by simply not being able to find something as quickly as you want to – how maddening it can be, for example, not to be able to lay your hands on the car keys first thing in the morning. What's actually going through your mind is not just the immediate frustration of not being able to locate something, but anxiety about all the possible knock-on effects:

● You can't find your keys
● So you'll be late getting to the station
● So you'll be late for work
● So you'll be late for a meeting
● So you may lose a client, a contract or goodwill with your boss . . .

Quite apart from ransacking your drawers, your trouser pockets and the internal sections of your briefcase over and over again being a complete waste of time, forgetfulness about where you put your keys can end up being a very damaging bit of inefficiency.

In day-to-day life, make sure you have done everything in your power to minimise the little stresses that can create a feeling of being out of control. **Time spent getting organised or setting up systems to make sure you always know where things are will pay off every time.** Putting up a few hooks for keys, having some kind of filing system for your personal papers, paying bills by direct debit so that when they get mislaid you don't get cut off, putting your address book on computer and having a diary which is up to date all sound pretty mundane, but think of this as an investment. If you haven't got to waste 15 minutes a day hunting for the various essentials that you need to run your life it means that you'll have more time and energy for other things. Who can honestly say that they don't spend at least a few minutes a day searching for things they can't function without – keys, mobile phone, diary? At 15 minutes a day, you are spending over 90 hours a year engaged in this futile activity; that's nearly four days a year down the drain. Go on, invest in a nail and nail down those essentials – it could change your life. And for every decade of your life, you'll have an extra month to play with.

The ideal is to avoid those situations that tend to cause you stress, or to look for a way around them. I used to find myself driving thousands of miles a year, and the stress of finding my own way to the destination, getting anxious about being late (and not wanting to fritter away time by being early) meant that I was always completely wound up by the time I arrived. There was a simple solution: I gave up driving. I discovered that flying, going by train or getting someone to drive me in a sane, relaxed manner meant that I was calm and ready to do business, and freed up the journey time for me to prepare or take it easy. It was a performance-enhancing solution and well worth the investment.

Spotting the difference between detail and trivia

Are those unanswered emails or the contents of your overflowing in-tray really important? Very often they are simply the cause of unnecessary stress. I found out just how much value most paperwork (and much electronic communication) really has in a rather dramatic way. In 1998, my sporting events company went through the extraordinary and devastating experience of being razed to the ground in a fire that blazed all night and smouldered on for a couple of days. Bizarrely it was on the anniversary of the Great Fire of London, and it caused the closure of much of central London. I was working in Jamaica at the time, and flew back as soon as I could to meet up with the staff. One of the managers, who ran a very large event that accumulated an immense amount of detailed paperwork, looked at me and smiled: 'Well, that's the filing done,' she said. For two weeks there was no in/out tray and no email. The lesson learnt was that anything that really requires attention will scream at us. The company was re-sited and was up and running again within five days. I know it's not always that simple, but the point is that we can become slaves to trivia. Now that we are contactable 24 hours a day, we need to be vigilant about the detail that matters and have mechanisms to filter out the dross from the detail.

Avoid fake props – you're grasping at straws

Very often we kid ourselves that some of the quick solutions to stress will solve the problem. Some of these props are not only ineffectual, they can be positively harmful and create side-effects of their own. The most obvious of these are alcohol and cigarettes, which many of us automatically reach for when we want to relax. Both of these actually stimulate the release of adrenalin. It is ironic then that the very supports we reach for to help us can actually have the opposite effect to the one we desire, making us even more stressed out than we were before. I know that lots of you won't want to hear some of this, but I have to cover the bases . . .

Cigarettes

Lots of people reach for a cigarette to make them relax, but nicotine actually increases adrenalin production, precisely what you don't need in order to wind down. Although no one reading this book will be unaware of the health problems associated with smoking (the government health warnings on poster advertising are pretty hard to miss, and if you can read this book, you've read the signs) it is probably worth noting some of the main ways in which 'Cigarettes can seriously damage your health':

- cancer of the lungs, larynx, bladder, kidneys, oesophagus, stomach and duodenum
- coronary heart disease
- bronchitis
- circulatory problems
- high blood pressure
- osteoporosis
- digestive disorders

(For more information on smoking see Appendices I, II and VI.)

Alcohol

It was quite literally a 'red'-letter day when research was published declaring that alcohol could be good for you. But only in strict moderation. One small glass of red wine a day is believed to have benefits for the heart and circulatory system – other types of alcohol and larger amounts of red wine, let's not kid ourselves, do us nothing but damage. As well as upsetting blood sugar levels and causing premature signs of ageing, excess alcohol damages the liver. What it certainly doesn't do is put us in control; quite the reverse, in fact. Taken in excess, alcohol tends to expose your underlying mental state to your colleagues, friends and family – if someone plies you with booze there is no way of controlling the outcome. As well as potentially ending up prostrate in front of your drinking companions (extreme, but it does happen), when you get to bed it's unlikely you'll be able to sleep. Alcohol can prevent you from reaching the level of deep sleep that the body needs in order to rejuvenate – hence its link with the ageing process. A further deterrent to overindulging should be the fact that alchohol is extremely high in calories – something many of us forget when we are knocking back a bottle of wine. So it's physical and emotional damage that we are opting for when we hang around in the pub for too long.

The best way to minimise a drinking habit is to:

- make the alcohol high quality
- resist feeling obliged to finish the bottle
- avoid drinking at lunchtime
- give your body a regular day off

Tea, coffee and cola

Caffeinated drinks give us an instant lift (they 'adrenalise' you), but have you noticed how short-lived it is? Soon afterwards, our energy level plummets. Caffeine has been shown to have a negative effect on the processing of certain kinds of information – so when you reach for a quick cup of coffee to make you more alert at your desk, you may be reaching for the very thing to dull your brain! Once again, this is a prop that gives you the diametrically opposite result to the one you want.

Chocolate, sweet snacks and junk food

When we are in a hurry it's very easy to grab some fast food or a sweet snack to give us energy. And it will, but, just like the drinks above, for a very limited time. These types of food, as well as containing very high proportions of chemical additives, preservatives, colouring and flavourings, also contain large amounts of fat and sugar. None of these things is good for your health and few of them contain very much real nutritional value. **These foods are simply a quick fix, and eaten in large quantities will make you fat and unhealthy and undermine your capacity to concentrate through the day**.

Drugs

In sport, although it's against the law, drugs are taken to enhance performance. But a career in professional sport is generally very brief, and retirement usually takes place before the side-effects of drug-taking have really set in. A well-known TV sports journalist in the US was alarmed by the number of footballers dying of unusual cancers, such as of the liver. She suspected that they had all abused steroids many years previously and she tried to get her network to make a documentary about the risks these sportsmen were taking. The network, however, was loathe to undermine the sport's clean image and, indeed, was so keen to protect its vested interest in football it refused to expose the scandal.

There are drugs that will give you the ability to work harder for short periods of time, but they cause untold damage along with a blurring of judgement. They are simply not worth it. Recreational drugs are all about escaping from reality – so that when you return to it, it all seems that much worse. Changing your reality to a more desirable one is a better, long-term solution.

Breaking habitual patterns of behaviour

The pressures around us, combined with our pressurised working environments, mean that we can quite easily get into a pattern of habitual behaviour and rely on the above-mentioned props, the most common and damaging of which are alcohol and cigarettes. Drunk to excess, alcohol is dangerous for both you and your relationships. You should make yourself aware of its dangers and ensure that you are in control of your drinking. You'll know for sure if you are hooked on cigarettes, and no doubt you'll be aware of all the methods of kicking the habit, from hypnosis, to patches, to reducing tar content until it's hardly worth lighting the match. If you manage to conquer your reliance on either alcohol or cigarettes, not only will you experience enormous physical benefits from 'spring cleaning' your body and a substantially reduced likelihood of some major diseases, but you will also give yourself an enormous sense of control. However, alcohol and cigarettes aren't the only addictions that can damage you. You may rely too heavily on other patterns of behaviour or props. **Ask yourself if there's anything in your life that you feel you can't do without. Even the good things, like exercise, taken to excess can be damaging and might need to be reined in.**

The real prop

While all those phoney props are waiting to tempt us, there is one genuine support for us all to grab. It requires something which is both underrated and has a bad name but is sometimes essential for you and for those around you: selfishness. Not just general selfishness (that would be disastrous) but selfishness in a very specific area: your **time**. Each day you must take time out that is entirely and exclusively for you. This is time that you should guard with your life – it *is* your life!

Think of it this way: your life is your software, held within a complex and valuable piece of hardware, and you need to look after both. The idea going through a renaissance at the moment that mind and body complement each other is not just a New Age, hippy notion. It was a theory first propounded by Hippocrates in the fifth century BC. The essential ingredient in this is time and thousands of years ago people discovered that time dedicated to looking after body and mind had major benefits for overall well-being.

Exercise

As well as burning up the excess adrenalin created by stress, exercise will make your body fitter and should extend your life. The enormous benefits of taking exercise (as well as advice on the different forms) will be dealt with in Chapter 3.

Social time

Being with other people – laughing, sharing ideas, sympathising, it doesn't matter which it is – provides huge emotional benefits.

Relaxation

You might achieve a state of relaxation through yoga, meditation, breathing exercises or simply listening to music. Whatever your method, relaxation is an essential part of unwinding and putting your life into perspective.

Sleep

Sleep is essential for the healthy functioning of the body. It allows the subconscious to release emotions (in the form of dreams) and gives bodily organs time to rest, recharge and regenerate.

Once you have decided to regain control, you have to start allowing yourself me-time. Everyone around you will benefit from the effects of this, so it is not really entirely selfish. Without this space for yourself you will lack the key to the vitality and energy that will defend you against all the potential problems in life. If your priorty has been to make money, now is the time to make time.

There is one environmental element in competitive swimming which is particularly crucial to performance. It's water temperature. If the water is too hot, you've got a problem because the body's cooling system has not evolved to work in hot water – it becomes impossible to work hard and you feel you're about to explode. Eventually you will pass out. Conversely, if the water is too cold, you will go numb, lose feeling and eventually lose consciousness. There is a narrow band of temperature that will enable you to excel in the water. If you are swimming over a short distance, the temperature can be a little higher, whereas a long distance swimmer will need a cooler temperature to ensure he doesn't overheat. Pressure is the equivalent 'environmental element' in your life. If you are under too much, you expose yourself to mental and physical breakdown. Conversely, if you have no pressure/stress at all you'll die – of boredom!

Action

- Have your diary to hand to remind you what's been going on in your life.
- Review your responses to Chapter 1's action points.
- Write down what you think makes your life too 'hot'.
- Make a list of people, situations or events that have been or are undermining your sense of control.
- Divide this list into two parts:
  - those that are self-inflicted,
  - those that are outside your control.
- List the action needed to control those that are self-inflicted:
  - confront?
  - negotiate?
  - avoid?
  - change?
- Repeat the process for those that are outside your control.
- List people or things that you have lost and are mourning.

- Identify a course of action that will allow you to come out of mourning.
- In your swimming lanes, list what gives you a sense of control, and what calms you and the waters you swim in.

CHAPTER 3

REACHING THE CREST OF A WAVE –

Step Three:
Look after your body

Maximising performance must be the guiding principle if we are to extract the most out of life. A one- or two-dimensional performance is not enough – only 3-D, full-technicolour will do. If you aspire to a 3-D performance, you will be adding texture, colour and depth to your life. **There is yet another, fourth, dimension however: the duration of your performance**. The longer you are able to deliver a satisfying performance, the more you will achieve. In this chapter, we'll look at how exercise and diet will give you the third dimension and how the fourth dimension – longevity – might develop from there.

A sporting goal

In sport you are always working towards a specific event, with your training geared to ensuring that you reach a peak of performance at a certain time, in a certain place, on a certain day. It takes this kind of focus and concentration to perform to your highest capability. When the stops are finally pulled out, all the different elements required to win should be in place.

Pitted against your peer group, your energy levels have to be raised to exactly the right pitch, and you have to be physically and mentally ready to win; if you are trained and prepared you will give your absolute optimum performance at this moment. You never hear of a sportsman quietly beating world record times in an informal practice session; athletes focus their efforts on achieving their ultimate performance when they are in a competitive situation and when the pressure of the moment will help push them to their furthest limit. They have 'named the day', and won't use up vital energy before it's really necessary. In the words of the Thorpedo (17-year-old Olympic gold medallist swimmer Ian Thorpe): 'You have to control all the controllables.'

So what's all this stuff about training and getting ready for an event got to do with you? Whether you are a shot-putter or a pen-pusher it has everything to do with you. Although the detail will be different, it is just as important for you to train and nourish your body properly as it is for an athlete. In your own field, you stand to achieve much more once you recognise that. Perhaps you don't think of your body as the vital element in how you earn your living, and, indeed, most readers of this book won't be male models or trapeze artists. Maybe your working life doesn't involve the use of any muscles apart from those in your right hand (to pen a signature or tap a computer keyboard) and those in your mouth (to give orders, make points at board meetings or drink cappuccinos). Perhaps the heaviest weight you ever have to lift is your fork at a business lunch and the only figure that matters is your quarterly profit. But maybe it's time for a review. **Last month's turnover might have been impressive, but are you as proud of your own vital statistics?**

Getting fit for the dream event

In Chapter 1, I talked about the importance of setting yourself specific goals, or 'dream events', to punctuate your life and give your landscape shape and texture. Inevitably, all these goals will require effort if they are worthwhile. They are the equivalent of the heats or matches that the athlete works towards. Your dream event is the equivalent of their sporting fixture, for which weeks, even months, of training and preparation will have specifically prepared them. In a sporting context three major elements influence your performance: your psychological state, your environment (which includes the people around you) and your physical skills and fitness. Whatever the context of your work, if you want to achieve anything beyond the minimum it's important to 'red line' certain moments or days for the fulfilment of your goals and to get your body and mind honed for that particular event. But, like the athlete, you can't just worry about your fitness and body weight the night before the race. Your physical condition has to be a priority *all* of the time, and you should know how and when that extra 10 per cent can be added for the days when you really need to be at your best.

Unless you're physically healthy and on top, it's unlikely that you'll be able to fulfil your potential in any area of your life, whether it's at work or at home. How can you, for example, achieve all you are capable of if you have had three colds in as many months and are hit by a migraine once a week. You'll be below par in the office and presumably semi-comatose at home. Even when you go on holiday you fall ill. Just like an athlete, who is entirely judged on his physical performance, you have to aspire to the level of fitness that will achieve your goals with the greatest ease and efficiency.

My red-letter day, 1976

For an athlete, the performance pressure points only come up once in a while. With the Olympics, for example, there's one chance every four years. At a squeeze, swimmers can make two Olympic Games, but usually it's only for one of them that they are at their physical peak, giving a single opportunity in a lifetime to win an Olympic Gold Medal. Though I had trained long and hard, I quite simply wasn't ready when I had my first opportunity at the 1976 games in Montreal. Nearly all the ingredients were there – probably 95 per cent in fact – but I couldn't quite pull my best performance together on the day.

All the work I had done over the past year was focused on one particular minute. The minute of the 100-metre breaststroke. All my training had been geared towards bringing my body to a peak for that race, and I felt like a well-agitated bottle of champagne about to burst into action once the restraining wire had been removed from the cork. As I wandered through the changing rooms and out into the warm-up area, I was totally preoccupied with my own thoughts. I lay down on one of the benches using my towel as a pillow and I could hear the Games in full swing on the other side of the glass partition. 'Why couldn't I swim now?' I asked myself. I was ready. But as I lay there with my eyes closed, I felt waves of fear rising up inside. Perhaps I'd peaked too early. I tried to stifle this negative thought but it kept rising up. At last it was time to go into the marshalling area, a glass tank of a room some six by three metres. It was soundproofed, and we could see out but no one could see in. There we were in the quiet of this room – the eight Olympic finalists – and we sat in profound silence for 40 minutes watching the monitors which showed what we could see clearly through the glass – gold medals being won and lost. Soon we would know who was Number 1 in the world.

I looked at the seven superb athletes I was about to swim against, and the eerie and funereal silence in the room grew and threatened to suffocate me. I could no longer look around me; I knew they would see the waves of naked terror on my face, and I felt sick to my stomach. I was a fake, a fraud. Perhaps it was just luck which had got me this far. Why should it be me who was one of the fastest in the world? Finally it was time, but my spirit was sinking and the last of my confidence drained away to be replaced by desperation. I felt as though I was clinging on to the last thread of my dignity. I'd come so far and it had cost me so much. 'I'll show them,' I said to myself.

As I stepped from the claustrophobic atmosphere of this glass coffin into the Olympic arena, I knew what it was like for the Christians emerging into the Colosseum to face the hungry lions. The pool deck was vast and deserted except for a few officials, and I suddenly felt very lonely. It was as though the eyes of the world were on me and there was nowhere to hide. At last, the whistle blew and we stepped up on our blocks. I had glanced across at David Wilkie, the other British swimmer in the race (and my arch rival), who was in the lane next to me. He was fiddling with his goggles but apart from that seemed totally unaffected by what was going on. 'I've got to prove myself to them,' I thought, and as the starting horn sounded I drove off the block with a rage in my body.

When I came to the surface I was clawing and tearing at the water, and as I came to the end of the pool I saw Wilkie touch the wall as I was turning. I was ahead of him but not by much. I knew I needed at least a metre lead to be sure of beating him. Ten metres to go – such a short distance. I tried to maintain my pace but I was drained. There was nothing left in me. With every stroke my body was becoming increasingly sapped of energy, and I knew I had wasted far too many of my valuable resources on those first few desperate strokes at the beginning of the race. I saw movement to my left. Wilkie. He was now ahead of me. My legs seemed to give up, but I pushed on – there was still the bronze medal. In the last few metres the water seemed to be sucking me back like an invisible current, preventing my dream from coming true. I lunged forward to touch the end and gasped for air, too exhausted to look at the scoreboard. When I did I saw John Henkens' name at the top. A new world record. Wilkie had got the silver and my name was well down the list in seventh place. Not even a personal best time. I'd had a baptism, however, a taste of the real thing. I'd been to the Olympic Games and I knew if I'd swum an hour earlier things would have been different. Next time I would be ready. Next time I would know what to expect.

In the course of your life, you will have plenty of opportunities to prove yourself, but you have to be fit and ready to do it. I had another opportunity four long years later, and then it was my minute and nobody else was going to have it. By then nothing was left to chance, all the details were covered. I had ironed out all my physical problems – and the psychological ones too – and I was absolutely ready to maximise my performance. Your red-letter days may not be so few and far between, but you still have to be fit and ready to do yourself justice.

MAXIMISING PERFORMANCE THROUGH EXERCISE

Achieving rock-hard buttocks and rippling biceps may be what motivates some people to pound the pavements and dangle the dumb-bells, but the benefits package actually includes some much more exciting items than bulging muscles – from experiencing a natural high to potentially extending the 'square end' of your life, by which I mean having a good quality, vigorous and virile life until the day you die.

The notion that you only need to be at your optimum fitness level if you run, jump or swim for your country or kick a ball for Arsenal is laughable. If you harbour that one, you need to shelve it right away. 'But I don't have time to exercise,' is the plaintive cry that often goes out from the sedentary mid-career male. My response to that is: *You don't have time not to!*

There are 168 hours in a week. Even allowing for eight hours sleep a night, **three exercise sessions of 45 minutes a week would take less than 2 per cent of your waking hours – hardly a large chunk of your time**. And even for just this small allocation of time, the benefits are enormous. It's as though you went off to the building society with £100 to invest and when you checked in your account a year later you had unexpectedly earned £1,000 in interest. A fairly minimal commitment can yield an unexpected and disproportionately large reward: on the emotional side, we reduce our levels of stress and anxiety. On the physical side, the cardiovascular, circulatory, digestive, lymphatic and respiratory systems all depend on activity for their healthy functioning. The British Heart Foundation recommends 30 minutes of moderate-intensity activity five times a week and says that the risk of coronary heart disease is substantially reduced for the physically active.(See Appendix III)

Your exercise objectives

If you are still unconvinced, or simply have a deep-rooted hatred of exercise, then keep reading. Perhaps you need further persuasion of the urgency. If you have an office-based job, for the best part of your waking hours your body is subjected to an occupation which is entirely unnatural: sitting. Behind a desk, on the train, at the dinner table, in front of the television. We even have whole rooms dedicated to the pursuit of sitting – as though most of us don't do enough of it without setting aside a special place to do a bit more! It always amazes me that people diligently take their dogs for a walk, but it wouldn't occur to them that they (or indeed their children) need exercise just as much as their canine companions – if not more.

If you want evidence that you weren't originally designed to be a full-time, long-distance, semi-professional sitter, simply observe a few of the most obvious and common effects of lack of exercise on your body: you get flabby, you become breathless running for the train, you can't do up your trousers. You can cultivate these symptoms in just a few weeks. Think about what will happen in a few months – or even years.

And what about the simple aesthetics of being overweight? It may have been a status symbol a couple of centuries ago (a large gut indicating that you were wealthy enough to live on rich foods, get moved around in a carriage and do a lot of reclining) but nowadays it has entirely different connotations. **If you want to be in control of your life, you have to be in control of your body.**

And lack of exercise, combined with the wrong diet, can have much more disastrous and long-term consequences. If you aren't motivated to do some exercise by the idea of feeling great, getting leaner and being younger-looking, then perhaps a look at the health problems associated with being overweight and under-exercised might persuade you to acquire a pair of running shoes. One of the most significant problems you may avert is heart disease. Believe me you wouldn't want to have a heart attack.

I was walking to work on a cold February morning in the year 2000 and didn't even notice the man walking towards me near St James's Park. What I did notice, however, was the chilling sound of a head, followed by a pair of glasses, hitting the pavement behind me. I knew what I would see when I turned around, so I had already started to reach for my mobile phone when I saw the surreal sight of a smartly dressed man lying flat on his back. I tried to undo his tie and top button and dropped my phone to focus on helping him. After several fumbling attempts I managed to check his breathing and put him in the recovery position. His breathing became more and more laboured, and stopped. He was dying and his lips had gone purple from lack of oxygen. Unless something was done immediately he wouldn't survive. No ambulance. Thirty-two years earlier I had taken a swimming life-saving award and vaguely remembered the routine. But I needed help. I asked a lady who had stopped to help by pushing on the man's chest when I instructed her, and, while I clasped his nose, we began mouth to mouth resuscitation. After inflating his lungs five or six times he gasped for air, and life returned. I then rolled him back into the recovery position and we sat waiting. It seemed like an age. I was so relieved to see the paramedics – it had been a long 11 minutes, and they worked on the man for some time. He had to be shocked at least three times by the defibrillator before he was loaded onto the ambulance. After giving a few details I continued on my way to work but found it hard to concentrate after having just watched someone so close to death.

A few weeks later I received a phone call. 'I am PC Sean Harper of the Royal Protection Unit,' a voice said. 'I was on duty when you saved a gentleman's life two weeks ago. He is a Member of Parliament and would like to thank you for saving the country the cost of a by-election.' Bob Sheldon is a splendid man, holding an extremely senior position in the Labour Government, and it has been a pleasure to get to know him. He tells me that you have a mere 5 per cent chance of surviving a cardiac arrest if you are not in hospital at the time, and your chance of recovery is around 80 per cent if a defibrillator is applied within the first two to three minutes after a heart attack. Apart from having no memory of the five days after the heart attack, he has made a complete recovery.

As well as heart problems, there are many other illnesses and diseases that you could be helping to prevent by taking exercise. This list should be enough to make you throw complacency off your agenda:

- high blood pressure
- diabetes
- osteoporosis
- circulatory diseases

(For more information see Appendices I and III.)

A healthy attitude to exercise

In the 1980s, getting fit was all about 'getting the burn'. Basically, if it didn't hurt like hell, it wasn't doing you any good. American journalist, Fran Lebowitz, observed rather drily: 'I look upon sport as dangerous and tiring, as activities performed by people with whom I share nothing except the right to trial by jury.' That's a pretty negative view of getting fit, but one you might well share if you ever stumbled by accident (or even design) into a high-impact aerobics class in the 1980s. The objective then was the body beautiful. The objective today is much broader. Taking part in any sport is better than doing nothing, except perhaps if you are a haemophiliac and fancy doing some bungee jumping – dangerous sports do not, on the whole, fit into the exercise framework I recommend to you.

Reaching for well-being

I described in Chapter 2 how extended periods of stress are likely to result in the body overproducing adrenalin, a side-effect of which is to make blood sugar levels unstable. The knee-jerk reaction to this is often to grab a quick-fix solution (tea, coffee or alcohol for example), but taking any of these stimulants is quickly followed by a further plummeting of energy as the pancreas produces insulin to bring the blood sugar level down. **This roller-coaster, if we don't make a concerted effort to get off it, will make our blood sugar swing from one extreme to another, with the longer-term consequences of exhaustion and ill health**. In this situation exercise burns off the adrenalin while increasing the blood supply that transports oxygen and nutrients to our cells. The end result is a real sense of well-being.

We run on two fuels – sugar and fat – and have two different kinds of muscle cells to burn them: the mitochondria for fat and the cytochrome system for sugar. As we age, however, there is a gradual atrophy of the mitochondria which makes us increasingly sugar reliant. The body can process sugar easily, converting it quickly and efficiently into energy, but since the body is also very sensitive to sugar levels, when they swing, our mood, concentration and performance suffer.

A further (and equally unwelcome) consequence of these sugar swings is middle-age spread. When blood sugar levels rise but don't get used up, the body has to deal with them – the famines that our ancestors experienced have conditioned our bodies not to waste a valuable resource such as sugar. When sugar levels become dangerously high, the body, through something called the glucogon reaction, converts blood sugar to fat, thereby storing the sugar for times of food shortage. The problem as we age is that the mitochondria cells atrophy and we are less able to burn this fat off – and so the bulge begins. Depressing? Yes, this is life, warts and all. Preventable? Thankfully yes.

Later in this chapter I will describe in more detail how to fuel yourself in order to largely mitigate sugar swings and reduce the likelihood of packing on weight, but this is only part of the equation. The other key lies within the mitochondria.

The role of the mitochondria and the cytochrome system

By unlocking the potential of the mitochondria and cytochrome system you not only stand to enjoy greater zest when you are older, but you'll also feel the benefit right now. If you counteract the atrophy of the mitochondria cells, your body will find it easier to regulate your sugar levels:

● So your energy levels will stabilise
● So your concentration will be enhanced
● So you will achieve more in all areas of your life
● So your confidence will increase
● So you will find it easier to achieve
● So you will have more time to do what you want
● So you will feel better about yourself and your life

If you are engaged in continuous movement over a long period of time, the cytochrome system will continue to call for sugar in the body. Eventually these sugars will run low as your stores are depleted and you will start to flag. If you are jogging, for example, your breath will become laboured and your body will tell you to stop. What is actually happening is that you are running out of sugar, and your body is reacting by releasing endorphins. This is like a switch: turn it on and the body will burn fat. The mitochondria now take over from the cytochrome system. Endorphins have other effects on your body. They assist respiration – as you jog, your breathing will become easier and smoother – and they are also a painkiller, so your body will become more comfortable. **Finally, endorphins give you a natural high, enhancing your sense of well-being. The pleasant effects of this linger for many hours after you have finished exercising**. Here's the positive cycle of exercise:

- As you exercise you burn the available sugar
- So you release endorphins
- So your breathing becomes easier
- So any pain you are suffering subsides
- So you feel great
- So you go back to your daily life energised
- So you find your tasks easier

Burning off adrenalin

Another major benefit of exercise is that it burns off excess adrenalin. If you have been under a lot of stress, exercise will make you feel more stable, and you will be able to think rationally about the complex day-to-day decisions you need to make. High levels of adrenalin interfere with sleep since you remain aroused during the night. As many of the businessmen I encounter are registering three times the normal level of adrenalin, sleep loss is almost inevitable. Once excess adrenalin has been burnt off, sleep becomes more restful and you stay for longer in the deep sleep phase in which the cells in your body are repaired. In addition to this, exercise causes a signal to be sent out by the muscles that they need building and repairing. This signal takes the form of polysaccharides, which tell the body to produce sterols. Sterols are responsible for maintaining bodily structures, and you may know them as steroids such as testosterone and oestrogen. They are the substances used illegally, either in their natural or synthetic form, by some athletes to enhance their physical performance (often dramatically).

Adrenalin forces the body into a state of physical readiness – like an engine it's revved up ready for the clutch to be dropped at the start of a race. Unfortunately for the body, however, if you don't exercise there is no race and the body will continue to rev. The stress this causes on your body is very undesirable and can lead to heart and blood pressure problems. Stress is also associated with an increased probability of cancer since adrenalin raises levels of oxygen in the blood, which appears to increase the number of oxygents and free-radicals in the system. These have been linked with cancer risk.

Without exercise and with high levels of adrenalin, your energy levels will flag, sleep will be intermittent and muscle tone will ressemble blancmange. **With** exercise, you set up the following positive chain reaction:

- As you exercise you burn sugar
- So you get rid of excess adrenalin
- So you get to burn fat
- So your muscles get fatigued and release polysaccharides
- So your body produces higher levels of hormones
- So your cells get repaired
- So this keeps you younger and in better condition
- So you operate better in all areas of your life

THE REWARDS OF EXERCISE

More stamina

Through exercise your muscles become increasingly efficient at using oxygen, thereby reducing the strain on the heart (itself a large muscle). In aerobic activity heavier breathing helps you to take more oxygen into your system, and the more you exercise, the more efficient the heart and blood vessels become at transporting oxygen-rich blood around your body. By increasing your physical stamina you increase your ability to cope with the pressures that you exert on yourself – and that others exert on you! Increasing your stamina is the key.

Greater strength

As you make more demands on your body through exercise, your muscles will become stronger and more developed – building strength is one way to make day-to-day tasks easier. Also, you need strong muscle groups to support the joints, so a knee joint, for example, that is only weakly supported by muscle, will wear (and wear out!) from the friction caused by unstable movement.

Increased suppleness

If your muscles are not stretched, they will shorten. This will restrict the movement of the joints, and muscles will tear more easily. Tight ligaments, tendons and muscles can create unwanted friction on the joints, causing joint erosion along with back and posture problems. Restricted mobility will make ordinary activities more difficult and even uncomfortable – imagine, if you couldn't even bend down to tie your own shoelaces, how reduced your quality of life would feel.

Strengthened immune system

Exercise supports the functioning of the lymphatic system, which helps our bodies fight infection: toxins are transported from our bodies via the lymphatic fluid in the lymph vessels to the lymph nodes (found at the neck, armpits and groin), and in turn these filter out impurities before taking the fluid back into the bloodstream. The whole system depends on the body moving in order to keep the lymph fluid flowing, so exercise plays a vital role in the process of detoxification.

Weight loss (and control)

Regular exercise can help with weight loss and with keeping your weight steady – running a mile, for example, will burn up to 300 calories (the calorie-cost of a small bar of chocolate or a pint and a half of lager). It can also help to increase the metabolic rate, which is the speed at which your body burns calories.

Improved control over appetite

Although you might suppose it to be the other way round, **people who exercise regularly find that they actually need to eat less . . . what a bonus!** It's tried and tested – if you don't believe me, when you next go for a run (not if!) notice how little temptation there is to dive into the biscuit tin on your return home.

Improved self-esteem

A fitter body, glowing skin, endorphins whizzing around – even the simple satisfaction of having got yourself out of an armchair and into a tracksuit – all these things improve self-esteem. Why be a slob when you have the chance to look better and feel better? How can you ignore such a powerful combination of benefits?

Improved brain power

Physical fitness is said to improve your brain power. The more balanced and fit your body, the theory goes, the more agile your brain will become. It is certainly true that after a good bout of exercise you can experience the most powerful feelings of mental alertness and sharpness, as though the connections between the brain cells are being more easily made. Some recent research has also suggested that exercise balances depleted supplies of glucose, making new ready-made fuel available to burn during mental effort. The one thing you certainly won't experience after exercise is mental sluggishness – it does quite literally 'clear your mind' and, as you often hear people say, makes you feel as though the cobwebs have been blown away.

Social side-effects

If you are playing a team sport, there is obviously the social aspect of exercise to be enjoyed. Even if you join a gym and do solitary weight training there can still be a strong sense of shared activity with those around you, and opportunities for socialising with like-minded people often arise.

Sex

It's probably not wise to think of sex as an alternative to exercise, however aerobic it may sometimes feel; only constant, uninterrupted action for 30 minutes a session, ideally five times a week, would be enough to save you the trouble of taking other forms of exercise. I am sure the odd celebrity would claim to be managing this, but let's be realistic, most of us aren't. **The really good news, however, is this: exercise increases your sex drive.** It does this in three ways: it boosts your hormone levels (testosterone is a hormone), it improves the workings of your body and it gives you more confidence in how you look – which inevitably improves your libido. So get your kit on – and I guarantee you'll feel better when you get your kit off.

In summary, by exercising regularly you will have a better balance of hormones cruising round your body along with more stable blood sugar levels. This, with all the other benefits we've described, will make you more energised and capable of achieving more in your life.

Getting started

Before you start any exercise programme, you should consult your GP. It is important that you take up activities which are right and safe for you, and only increase them gradually, both in time and in intensity. **A full medical and physical stress test will provide a starting point and give you something against which to measure your improvement.**

What type of exercise is best?

For the complete bag of performance-enhancing benefits, endurance exercise is the key. By this I mean exercise that doesn't involve stopping and starting. The second you stop, your cytochrome system begins to recharge with sugar and you then return to your starting point. It is only when you have depleted the cytochrome system of sugar that endorphins kick in and your mitochondria start burning fatty acids. Rugby, football and cricket are all stop-start games, so if you have played these sports, continuous exercise over long periods may be something new to you.

Beyond the physiological ability simply to keep going, the main challenge of endurance exercise is the defeat of boredom. And I'd be the first to admit it – it's not easy to motivate yourself until you start to enjoy the huge benefits which the habit of exercise can bring you. It is vital to keep going, however: even if you jog it will take ten to 12 minutes to burn the readily available sugar supply before you feel the endorphin surge, and you then need to continue for a further ten to 12 minutes to reap the full benefits.

Whatever form of exercise you take up, you should feel comfortable with it. I tend to mix around what I do and change my routine every six months. In summer, playing sports outdoors adds another dimension. I sometimes recommend tennis. Although it is a stop-start game, it does have an added social dimension, and if you get some coaching every other week you will have the incentive to get into better all-round shape in order to feed the improvement in your game. Indeed, you could penalise yourself by going for a run instead of playing tennis if you have failed your three-times weekly training commitment.

As I said, I vary the exercise I take, but it would be remiss of me not to swing my swimming bias at you. Swimming is an exceptional sport that assaults your senses like no other, improving your stamina as well as enhancing suppleness and flexibility. Furthermore, when or if other exercise becomes a problem later in life, you can usually still swim.

When making your choice, think **legs**. Not because you'll probably have to wear shorts, but because your largest muscle groups are from your waist down. **So whatever exercise you do, think legs and work legs as they will burn more of your fuel reserves**.

Make sure you take as much exercise in the winter as in the summer – hibernation is not an option, nor is taking a sabbatical from your fitness regime.

Impact exercise

Aerobics and jogging are termed 'impact' exercise – not to be confused with impact sports. The impact referred to is your foot hitting the ground and catching the downward momentum of your body. The shockwaves this sends through your muscles, and the effort of stopping the downwards momentum, burns more fuel. You can grasp this concept by trying to jog slowly down a steep hill. The breaking is tiring and difficult, and is the reason why impact exercise tends to burn more energy and therefore get you to the fat burning mode faster than other kinds. The down side is that the impact causes a lot of wear and tear on your joints.

Where and what will suit you?

Before plunging headlong into a fitness programme, you have to consider what sort of exercise will actually suit you. Everyone has different criteria, varying amounts of time and activities that they like or hate intensely. Jogging might be your idea of a nightmare, punishing yourself in a gym with 30 other sweaty bodies somebody else's.

Consider the following:

- Do you want to exercise at home with some domestic gym equipment or a video?
- Do you want to exercise in a gym or at a leisure centre?
- Do you want to exercise indoors or outdoors?
- Do you want to exercise first thing in the morning, in your lunchtime or in the evening?
- Do you like competitive sport?
- Do you prefer sport requiring individual rather than team effort?
- Do you want your exercise to include a social element?
- Do you need an exercise partner?
- Do you need motivation from a personal trainer?
- Do you want your exercise to be entirely free (apart from the cost of the appropriate shoes) or are you prepared to pay out?

It is important to answer these questions before you rush out and pay £750 to join a flashy gym, thinking that simply by writing a cheque you'll make yourself hunky and handsome. How do you think most gyms make their profits? Lots of them do it by selling memberships in the first week of January to people who have no staying power. None whatsoever. **Lured by the guilt of seasonal overeating and the short-lived power of the new year's resolution, men queue up at the gym in their droves with joining fees in hand, only to fall by the wayside a few months later.** From March to December, their scarcely worn trainers and designer singlets do nothing but grow mould at the back of the cupboard. Does this sound familiar?

The single most important thing about taking exercise (apart from checking up with your doctor that you are fit enough to do it) is to *stick at it*.

Whatever activity you take up:

- It has to be one activity (or perhaps a choice of several) which you do at least three times a week, with almost religious regularity.
- It should be convenient, so that you never have to make excuses about why you can't manage to do it.
- It should be an activity that you are prepared to persevere with.
- It should be one that you can sustain while you are travelling – always make sure there are fitness facilities at your hotel.
- It has to be made an absolute priority, with dates inked in your diary in letters as large as the entries that say: 'Board meeting', 'Dinner with clients', 'Staff pay reviews'. **Make sure your diary entries for exercise are respected – not bumped**.

How long should you exercise?

Always warm up with some light exercise and then do some stretching. To begin with, don't exercise for long, because if you wake up too stiff you might be tempted to use it as an excuse for missing your next work-out. Each time you exercise, work yourself a little harder until you are doing 25 minutes of jogging or at least an hour of brisk walking (impossible in a city, where you will keep having to cross roads). This is equivalent to 40–45 minutes on a static bike. Finish with a warm-down by gradually reducing the level of effort and doing some stretching, sit-ups and back strengthening exercises (if you have a back problem, seek medical advise first). You may also wish to lift weights to build the muscle groups which have not been exercised on, for example a static bike.

How hard should you work?

Surprisingly, it's not that hard to get the full, fat-burning gains. You need to be exercising at the level where you can still have a conversation. This may sound rather pedestrian, and you may be tempted to run faster, but remember, we are meant to be gently servicing the body, not thrashing it! If you are injured or ill you must rest your body and allow it to recover, unless your doctor has specifically told you otherwise.

Getting over the boredom

It's hard to avoid the boredom of endurance exercise unless it's part of a master plan like going for a gold medal. I'm not training for that any longer so I focus on the benefits of how I feel before, during and particularly afterwards – it certainly reinforces why I suffer the drudgery. Unless you are one of the lucky ones who really enjoy rhythmic exercise and find it soothing and unwinding, you may need to distract yourself with music, TV or reading.

When do you exercise?

If the evening is your chosen time, make sure you don't leave it too late – as the night wears on, your resolve might ebb; exercising late at night may also make sleeping difficult. The important thing is to find the slot that suits you – and make it a ritual to work out at that particular time.

Getting your system in gear

Unlike a car, which comes back from the garage purring, the body takes time to respond and the benefits of exercise will not be felt immediately. If your body has been under-used, fat may have started to build up and muscle to atrophy. Like an engine, the body runs on fuel. It needs oxygen and a spark from the brain to get going, but with too much unused oxygen forced in by a persistently adrenalised state, the body will take time to 're-tune'. **If you have been completely sedentary, it will** take something like three weeks to get it to respond to the wake-up call. Muscle strength will then start to return and the cardiovascular system to strengthen. Endorphins will flow more easily, burn-up of adrenalin will allow freer flow of serotonin to the brain, and the rate at which the blood carries oxygen into the lungs will increase. Expulsion of unwanted by-products from your muscles will improve and your cooling system will be more responsive; the evidence of this will be that you will break into a sweat more easily. In fact your whole system will be more responsive to movement. Your weight might initially increase (as muscle weighs more than fat), and if you have called upon the spare fuel tank of fat around your body, you may well have retained fluid. Slowly the body will react and adjust to your new lifestyle, using up reserves and dumping unwanted fluid. This will not be a smooth process but, with patience and perseverance, you may find you can trade in the old banger for something a bit more like a Ferrari – perhaps not the latest model, but something that has at least a small chance of turning heads.

Sell your partner the benefits

If you have a partner, I shall assume you want to spend the rest of your life with her. You then both have the right and the responsibility to look after your health and fitness. That doesn't mean being a keep-fit bully or bore! Selling by example worked for me: my wife saw the huge benefits I was enjoying from regular work-outs and wanted some of the action. Now we take time out to exercise together, and it adds another very rewarding dimension to our lives.

MAXIMISING PERFORMANCE THROUGH FOOD AND NUTRITION

You are what you eat

Another key to getting your body into optimum condition so that you can fulfil all your aims and ambitions is of course to pay attention to what you eat. The general rule for most of us is that we should exercise more and eat less. It's quite a simple recipe, and once you have some good habits, it doesn't necessarily entail great self-denial.

(See Appendix IV)

Diets don't work – good habits do

To many of us, the word 'diet' simply means 'losing weight', and has unwelcome connotations of guilt, deprivation and, quite often, failure (not unlike the effect of the word 'exercise' on some people!). 'Imprisoned in every fat man a thin one is wildly signalling to be let out,' said Cyril Connolly. I suppose this is true, but there are an awful lot of them who aren't signalling very effectively – and if they are it isn't doing much good.

There are plenty of dieting blind alleys. **If you do need to lose some weight, the worst thing you can do is miss meals – particularly if you have to function normally, even more so if you have a red-letter day looming and you need to maximise performance.** If your body is deprived of food, your liver will release glucose directly into the bloodstream in order to supply you with some energy. At best, this leads to jitteriness and at worst a feeling of panic. What's the first thing we do when we feel like this? Reach for an instant sugar hit. Since a bar of chocolate is often the fastest way to lay our hands on something sweet, bang goes the diet.

Drastic calorie-cutting diets are similarly counter-productive. If you inflict a sudden low-calorie diet on your body, the reduction will be perceived as a threat and your metabolic rate will slow down by anything up to 45 per cent. This means that you will actually take much longer to burn up the calories in anything you eat. The clever deception is that on a diet of this kind you might quickly lose several pounds at the beginning. This, however, is mostly body fluid, which will return when you start eating normally. Then there are all the food fad diets, where you eat cabbage soup, kidney beans or perhaps pineapples in vast quantities until you are screaming for mercy. Once again, you are likely to reach for chocolate or doughnuts or almost anything self-indulgent to break the monotony.

If you have tried unsuccessfully to shed a few pounds and decided it's all too much effort (or you know you should but can't quite be bothered while you can still just about do up your trousers), you should stop and think a bit more about what food actually does for you. Your 'diet' is your fuel and it's the quality of the fuel you should be concerned about as much as the quantity. Would you even dream of putting leaded petrol in a car which took unleaded? Of course not. But some of the junk food we fill ourselves with is probably doing just as much damage. If you want a decent performance out of your body, you need to make sure that it's getting the best. Your body has the potential to be a high-performance vehicle. Treat it like one. **What you eat can make a huge impact on your general health, energy levels, brain power, immunity from illness, longevity and, last but not least, weight.** Examine the various jobs food does for your body and re-educate yourself to eat the right things.

What is food made up of?

Foods are divided into three essential types: carbohydrates, fats and proteins. To function properly, our bodies also require vitamins, minerals and fibre, which are contained in varying amounts in the foods we eat day-to-day – that is if we are eating a healthy, balanced diet.

Many of us, however, are not. Most of us probably have a vague idea of the foods which are really bad for us – even if that knowledge is based on the nasty after-taste which is left by slimey take-aways, greasy chips and pork scratchings, and that feeling that we wish we hadn't eaten them. We know much less, however, about which foods are good for us and why. In Western society we have moved towards patterns of eating where the balance between the three chief food groups (protein, fats and carbohydrates) has drastically altered. Thousands of years ago, our diet comprised approximately: 70 per cent carbohydrates, 15 per cent fat and 15 per cent protein. That was more or less ideal. Today, a more typical composition is 50 per cent carbohydrates (of which 20 per cent is sugar), 40 per cent fat and 10 per cent protein. This is a pretty drastic change and not one that our bodies have adapted to particularly well. And it's not just what we eat. It's how we eat and when. In more primitive times, we 'grazed'; we ate when we found food (little and often), and we ate it raw. Our blood sugar was kept even and presumably our energy, moods and concentration were much more consistent. Nowadays lifestyles are geared towards fewer, larger meals, made from refined ingredients and cooked using any one of about a 100 different methods. This gives our bodies a whole set of different problems to contend with.

What the food groups do for you and where they are found:

Carbohydrates:
- needed for energy
- found in fast-releasing form in such foods as sugar and honey, and in refined foods such as biscuits and white bread
- found in slow-releasing form in complex carbohydrates such as whole grains, pulses, vegetables and fruit

Fats:
- needed for energy and to help growth and repair
- saturated fats are found in meat and dairy products
- unsaturated fats are found in olive oil, nuts, seeds and fish

Proteins:
- needed for growth and repair of body tissue
- found in fish, meat, dairy products and vegetables

Fibre:

- needed to prevent constipation and, by keeping bowel content moving, to reduce the likelihood of bowel cancer (by stopping the formation of cancer-forming toxins by the bacteria which live on waste products)
- found in fruit, vegetables and wholegrains

What vitamins do for you and where they are found:

Vitamin A

- needed for the immune system, protection against some cancers and healthy skin
- found in liver, vegetables (especially broccoli, cabbage, carrots, pumpkin and watercress) and fruit (especially melon, apricots and tangerines)

Vitamin B

The B vitamins are: B1 (thiamin), B2 (riboflavin), B3 (niacin), B5 (pantothenic acid), B6 (pyridoxine) and B12 (cyanocobalamin).

- needed for the release of energy from food, healthy functioning of the nervous system, ability to deal with stress, good circulation, a strong immune system and healthy skin, hair and eyes
- found in varying quantities throughout a balanced diet including plenty of fresh vegetables (especially broccoli, cabbage, tomatoes and watercress) and dairy products, wholegrains, poultry and nuts

Vitamin C

- needed for the immune system, tissue repair and protection against cancer and heart disease

- found in cabbage, citrus fruit, potatoes and tomatoes

Vitamin D

- needed for strong and healthy bones
- found in mackerel, salmon and eggs

Vitamin E

- needed for cell protection, skin repair and immune system function
- found in beans, sunflower seeds, tuna and wheatgerm

Vitamin K

- needed for blood clotting
- found in Brussels sprouts, cauliflower, peas and watercress

Minerals

In addition to the vitamins above, the human body requires a number of minerals. Those required in larger quantities are: calcium (vital for bone strength and density), magnesium (helps with bone density and muscle strength), sodium (for maintaining water concentration in the blood and for muscle impulses), and potassium (works with sodium).

Those required in smaller quantities – but which are no less important – are: iron (instrumental in carrying oxygen and carbon dioxide to and from cells), chromium (for glucose tolerance), manganese (to work against free radicals and for brain function), selenium (for cancer protection) and zinc (to help boost the immune system).

How we devitalise our food

In spite of the fact that we now know a great deal about what all our available foodstuffs contain and the function of all their different nutritional elements, we have simultaneously developed a number of ways of completely knocking the goodness out of them. How perverse can you get?

Here are some of the ways in which we inflict damage on the foods we eat and deprive them of their potential value.

Storing – from picking to eating

Some vitamins are destroyed by exposure to air and light, so the longer we keep foods that contain them, the less goodness will be left in them. Think of your average supermarket apple. A Granny Smith which has been put in a crate, transported half way round the world, wrapped in cellophane, left lurking on a supermarket shelf for a few days and sat decoratively in your fruitbowl on the window ledge for another week will give you very different nutritional benefits from an apple picked from a tree in a garden and eaten moments later. Foods deliver much more nutritional value if they are fresh – and kept in the cool and dark.

Spraying – putting off the pests

Chemical spraying kills pests, but it also makes crops less nutritious for human consumers. Some of the chemicals used have been proved to be carcinogenic, toxic to the brain and damaging to the nervous system; association has also been made with depression, memory decline, migraine and other ailments. Since chemicals can penetrate well below the surface of fruit and vegetable skins, even scrubbing or peeling may not be sufficient to remove the harmful elements, hence the understandable growth in demand for organic produce. If you are going to eat plenty of fresh fruit and vegetables, as all nutritionists advise, they may as well be doing you more good than harm! I always buy organic fruit and vegetables where they are available.

Refining – knocking out the goodness

Many of our foodstuffs are so refined that all the good parts have been eliminated. White bread, processed cereals and white rice may appeal to our sophisticated Western palate, but they have been stripped of their nutritional value and, even if eating them provides us with some short-lived energy, they are otherwise 'empty' calories, giving us nothing of real, lasting benefit. Think wholemeal bread, demerara sugar, porridge and brown rice.

Eating on the run – a health hazard
The biggest danger in walking along while eating your chips is not that you might trip over the kerb, it's what the chips themselves are doing to your system. Frying adds large amounts of fat to any food, giving it a very high calorie content but little nutritional value per calorie. Most fast foods are made with more fat, sugar and chemical flavourings than can possibly be good for us, and the same goes for many ready-made meals, which have sell-by dates light-years ahead. If we rely on these to keep ourselves going, we can find ourselves eating more preservative than protein. You should keep your intake of fast and convenience foods to a minimum – eating them is tantamount to filling a Rolls Royce with 2-star petrol.

Fatty and fattening – or raw and real
We have a choice with most raw ingredients – either to maximise or minimise their nutritional content. Using excessive cooking fat, adding creamy sauces, sprinkling liberally with salt and overboiling can all help to create dishes which are fattening, energy-draining and heart-attack-inducing. Cooked in other ways, the same ingredients can play a role in giving us health and vitality. Whether you are cooking at home or picking from a menu, go for the lightly stir-fried, steamed or poached options. It's worth remembering that **the nearer vegetables are to their raw state, the more vitamins and nutrients they retain**.

Supplementing with pills

Whether or not you need to supplement your diet with vitamin and mineral supplements is debatable. If you ate healthily with plenty of fresh and organic produce and lived in a pollution-free environment in a stress-free world, your body would probably be getting everything it required without the need to resort to the galaxy of pills and potions now available on the market. Most of us do not live in this ideal world and don't always have time to chop up organic vegetables and lightly steam them with some freshly caught fish. If you think your diet is lacking in any particular area (perhaps due to illness, lifestyle or predisposition) you should discuss with your doctor whether to compensate for any deficiency by taking supplements. He or she will advise you on the recommended daily allowance for you and in what form you should take it.

Your diet can also influence the amount of cholesterol in your blood and therefore the risk of heart attack. You should therefore have this checked by your doctor and if necessary seek advice on whether medication or a change in diet is needed to balance this.

Patterns of eating – how to maximise your energy

Broadly speaking, you should avoid foods that give you a fast rush of energy, as this boost will be followed by a dip – and shortly afterwards by a craving for the next rush. As the sugar we eat makes our blood sugar level rise, the pancreas produces insulin in order to bring the level down again. Each time we reach for a sugary snack, the pancreas is set to work once again, and this over-use can eventually leave it unable to function. Biscuits, cakes, chocolate and fizzy drinks all contain highly refined ingredients which require little work to be broken down by the body, allowing sugar to be released into the bloodstream very swiftly. Fresh fruit, on the other hand, contains a natural sugar called fructose which is released more slowly into the system and won't 'let us down' in the way that refined foods do.

Comparative effect on your energy levels between fast-release food (e.g. chocolate) and slow-release food (fruit and veg)

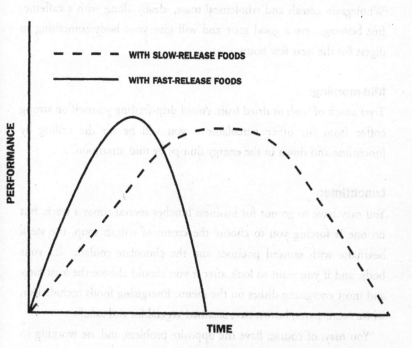

To give your body a chance to be energetic and your mind a chance to be focused, you need to fuel yourself on a fairly regular basis with the right foods (and drinks). Here are a few very basic guidelines:

Breakfast:

Many people (and I think men are particularly prone to this) boast that they never eat breakfast. They spend so much time shaving carefully, choosing a tie and finding matching cufflinks that there is no time to sit down to a bowl of branflakes before rushing off for the train. This is a mistake. Breakfast quite simply sets you up for the day, and you should never go without it. **If you miss breakfast you are much more likely**

to grab some strong coffee and a pastry in the middle of the morning, because you simply can't make it until lunchtime. Wholegrain cereals and wholemeal toast, ideally along with a caffeine-free beverage, are a good start and will give your body something to digest for the next few hours.

Mid-morning:

Try a snack of fresh or dried fruit. Avoid drip-feeding yourself on strong coffee from the office percolator – you will be on the ceiling by lunchtime and down in the energy dumps by mid afternoon.

Lunchtime:

You may have to go out for business lunches several times a week, but no one is forcing you to choose the cream of stilton soup, the steak bearnaise with sautéed potatoes and the chocolate roulade. It's your body, and if you want to look after it you should choose the least fatty and most energising dishes on the menu. Energising foods include fish, white meat, pasta, brown rice, steamed vegetables and salads.

You may, of course, have the opposite problem and are working so hard that you don't have time for lunch. This is almost as bad as overdoing it in a Michelin-starred restaurant. Both kinds of behaviour will leave you functioning below par for the rest of the day. Missing lunch will mean that you have no energy for the afternoon – and again you'll be more likely to boost yourself with black coffee, biscuits and chocolate. There is no day so busy that it can't be punctuated for a sandwich – wholemeal bread with a filling such as tuna or chicken and some fruit is enough to fuel you for a few hours.

Mid-afternoon:

Have some fruit – it will keep you going until dinner.

Evening meal:

Conventional wisdom tells us to breakfast like a king, dine like a prince and sup like a pauper. There are, of course, people who manage to feast on a large dinner and still get a good night's sleep – but I'm not one of them. If I eat too much heavy food too late in the day, my body is unable to relax at night, so in the evening I avoid pasta, rice and potatoes and opt for extra portions of vegetables. There are some foods that are said to have a sedative effect so if you need to eat late but want a restful night you could try; avocados, bananas, oranges or peanut butter.

If you want to boost yourself in a specific area, here are a few pointers:

Under STRESS?

If you are under great stress your body will benefit from a Vitamin C boost so make sure that you eat plenty: oranges, lemons, kiwi fruit, red peppers, tomatoes and leafy vegetables are all good sources.

Feeling BLUE?

Depression can be exacerbated by a lack of calcium and magnesium so make sure you are eating plenty of fresh and dried fruit, root vegetables, pulses and nuts. Also check that you are keeping your iron intake up; good sources are red meat, shellfish and poultry.

Need to WIND DOWN?

Complex carbohydrates can increase serotonin levels in your brain which are known for their calming and soothing effects. Eat them in the form of rice, noodles, couscous and potatoes.

Lacking ENERGY?

Eating foods which are digested fast and efficiently is one way to lift your energy – fresh and raw fruit and vegetables are a good source. Add some protein to these (eggs, yoghurt, cheese, fresh fish, chicken and lean meat) and you'll be raring to go.

Risk being the WEAKEST LINK?

Improve the sharpness of your brain and memory function by making sure you have plenty of the following: B vitamins (broccoli, asparagus, brown rice and oily fish for example), minerals (found in wholegrains, bread, cereals and fish) and iron (red meat, shellfish and poultry).

If you are eating a balanced diet, taking in a good mix of all the different food groups, you'll be giving yourself the best chance of finding a true and sustainable sense of well-being and enhanced performance.

What to drink

I have already tried to encourage you not to grab tea, coffee and fizzy drinks as your thirst-quenchers or energy-boosters. They will have the reverse effect. Alcohol has also been covered in the previous chapter, but it is worth recalling here that alcohol drastically lowers your ability to perform in any situation, from the office to the bedroom. Even if you use it to gain confidence, the result will probably not be the one you hoped for. The best drink is water.

We've all heard the expression 'dull as ditchwater', and oddly enough that's just how I feel about a two-litre bottle of still mineral water, which is the approximate, recommended daily dose. At least ditchwater might have a flavour. But when you look at what is promised if you really do spend the day sipping, you might change your mind.

Water helps you to:

- eliminate toxins by flushing out the liver
- prevent constipation (which is often due to a lack of fluid in the intestine)
- prevent headaches
- prevent bad breath
- boost your energy
- get rid of dark shadows under your eyes
- promote glowing skin

You don't have to drink two litres of water all in one go – in fact that would be pointless under normal circumstances. If you drink it in small quantities throughout the day (a glass at breakfast with a twist of lemon, some diluted fruit juice during the day, a few cups of herbal tea and several glasses with each meal) you will easily get through it, and, given that many foodstuffs have a high water content, (e.g. salad and fruit) within a fairly short time you should see and feel some results. There are arguments for and against drinking bottled water versus tap water and it's probably worth seeking advice on the tap water in your own area before making a decision about this.

The broad rules, therefore, are to:

- eat small, regular meals
- eat plenty of raw or lightly cooked vegetables
- cut down on red meat and opt for fish or poultry
- avoid 'empty' calorie food
- choose wholegrain and unrefined options where available
- avoid over-consumption of fats
- avoid skipping meals

- avoid eating late at night
- drink plenty of water

By making a few positive resolutions about taking exercise and eating a healthy diet, you will be taking significant steps towards promoting your body's optimum health and energy. Increased energy levels and improved, all-round fitness play an essential role in helping you achieve your goals, whether they are physical, intellectual or emotional. **Quite simply, if you feel good, you will also feel that anything is possible – and if you feel anything is possible, you will be strongly motivated to succeed.**

The fourth dimension – looking forward to the square end

We tend to accept that that we will suffer a remorseless decline in body, mind and spirit as we age. But there are older people who keep their diet and exercise regime well controlled, have a high level of interest in life and are active physically and mentally well into their eighties and nineties. Of course there is a genetic element in all this, but you can also do a lot to promote this state of health and fitness – and you'll feel the benefits right from the start and for decades to come. We all know a few young but old people – the marketing men have christened them the 'grey panthers' – they are pensioners with income, attitude and a zest for life and new challenges.

As we look around us and see the consequences of the life decisions that people we know have made, it should become abundantly clear that quality of life beyond middle age is all a matter of choice:

Choice one: an uncomfortable tailing off in which movement turns into hard labour and doing up your shoe laces becomes an extreme sport. This is to suffer gradual decline.

Choice two: strength, agility, flexibility and endurance are maintained. This is to enjoy the 'square end' of life.

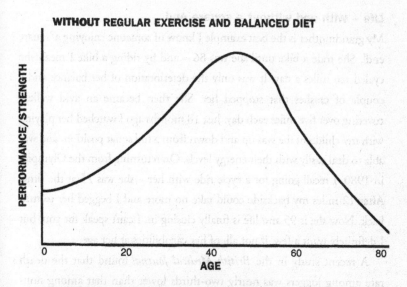

WITHOUT REGULAR EXERCISE AND BALANCED DIET

PERFORMANCE/STRENGTH

0   20   40   60   80

AGE

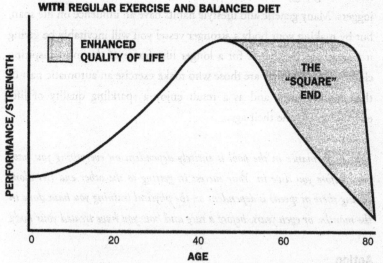

WITH REGULAR EXERCISE AND BALANCED DIET

ENHANCED
QUALITY OF LIFE

THE
"SQUARE"
END

PERFORMANCE/STRENGTH

0   20   40   60   80

AGE

The square end, as you can see from the illustration, is the opposite of the gradual decline. Having a square end to your life means being able to continue all the physical and social activities you enjoy in your thirties and forties well into your fifties, sixties, seventies — even eighties and nineties.

Life – with and without a square end

My grandmother is the best example I know of someone enjoying a 'square end'. She rode a bike until she was 86 – and by riding a bike I mean she cycled ten miles a day. It was only the deterioration of her balance and a couple of crashes that stopped her. She then became an avid walker, covering over five miles each day. Just 18 months ago I watched her playing with my children; she was up and down from a full squat position, and was able to deal easily with their energy levels. On returning from the Olympics in 1980, I recall going for a cycle ride with her – she was 75 at the time. After 12 miles my backside could take no more and I begged her to turn back. Now she is 95 and life is finally closing in. I can't speak for you, but I definitely want a few, if not all, of her capabilities at her age.

A recent study in the *British Medical Journal* found that the death rate among joggers was nearly two-thirds lower than that among non-joggers. Many genetic and lifestyle habits have an influence on life span, but by making your body a stronger vessel you will inevitably be giving it a much better chance for a longer life. Some of the most inspiring elderly people I know are those who make exercise an automatic part of their daily routine and as a result enjoy a sparkling quality of life, enviable in anyone their age.

Your performance in the pool is entirely dependent on everything you have done before you dive in. Your success in getting to the other end (let alone getting there at speed) is dependent on the physical training you have done in the months, or even years, before a race and how you have treated your body.

Action

- Review your responses to Chapter 2's action points.
- Weigh yourself and enter your weight in your pad.
- Pick the suit in your wardrobe that currently fits you best and make a note of it in your pad.

- Book in for a full medical and physical stress test now.
- Write down the results of your tests so that you can refer back to them.
- Book your next appointment for twelve months' time.
- Plan your new exercise regime and put it in your diary.
- List what changes you are going to make in your diet: what will there be less of and what will there be more of?
- If appropriate, set a modest amount of weight to lose in the next six months.

CHAPTER 4

KEEPING YOUR HEAD ABOVE WATER

Step Four: Create Balance in Your Life

'All work and no play makes Jack a dull boy.' I loved that saying when I was a child. It made me feel much better about not liking school work, and I enjoyed the reminder to those who swotted too hard that they might get boring if they never took their heads out of their books.

This saying has far more relevance, however, for adults than for kids. As children we have a natural instinct for play, and even those who excel in the classroom feel the an urge to put their books to one side and go and muck around outside. But the mid-career man needs to be reminded: 'Being in the office for 14 hours a day and not having any interests outside work makes Jack an exceedingly dull man.' It makes him dull to his friends, his family and even to himself. Since the average man is under considerable pressure to perform in the office and to deliver the fruits of his labours to his family, it isn't really surprising that so many men get hooked by this one, and simply can't extricate themselves. They get locked into a career which demands increasingly more out of them as time progresses and stuck into a set of ever-growing financial commitments (mortgage, school fees, expensive holidays, etc.) which tie them more and more firmly to the job.

Often the occasional 12- to 14-hour day (initially perceived as an exception – to achieve specific deadlines perhaps) starts to become a routine. From being a routine it becomes a habit, until leaving the office at 9 or 10 p.m. is felt to be the norm and leaving at 5.30 p.m. causes eyebrows to be raised. If it is endemic in the company culture that employees work these sorts of hours, then cracks will start to appear, not just in the individuals but in the corporation as a whole. **Those who work from when it gets light in the morning to several hours after it gets dark (and perhaps a few hours over the weekend too) have quite simply lost the plot.**

There are many reasons why people get into the habit of voluntarily working the kind of hours that European Union law now regards as a violation of human rights, and if you find yourself saying (or even thinking) any of the following, you have a problem that needs to be addressed:

'My job is so important it needs 150 per cent commitment.'

Bertrand Russell wrote: 'One of the symptoms of approaching nervous breakdown is the belief that one's work is terribly important. If I were a medical man I should prescribe a holiday to any patient who considered his work important.' Clearly our work should be worth doing, and if it's not we should change job to one that has a better fit with our skills. It's quite another thing, however, to regard it as a matter of life and death (unless we are in the medical profession) or of national importance (unless we are senior members of the Cabinet). Keep your job in perspective and always remember that it is only one aspect of your life, not the be all and end all of your existence.

If you have a tendency towards spending too much of your time in the office, the growing trend among large corporations to make things comfortable for their staff will only increase it – and you should be wary. Gyms and swimming pools get installed in the office basement, in-house acupuncture is offered in the lunch hour and there are cappuccinos on tap in the 'break out' (formerly 'staff') room. The danger of providing recreational facilities within the four walls of the office building is of course that the division between working time and leisure time gets conveniently blurred, often for the benefit of the company. Even the 'dress down' trend can soften the old distinctions between home and work, and when you add in the mobile phones provided by your employer (meaning that you're always available, any time of day or night), there's hardly a moment or an area of your life that the office hasn't stealthily colonised. Even if the motive is not always selfish, the net result of all these changes to the traditional nine to five working pattern is that employees spend even more of their waking hours working.

One client of mine was particularly enthusiastic about the introduction of European law on working hours. He saw it as his saviour, since he was addicted to his treadmill and felt unable to get himself off it. Although the corporation he worked for did not require (or even expect) him to work the number of hours he did, there was an atmosphere of insecurity that kept him chained to his desk. Over the years I watched the corrosive effect on him of living on adrenalin. Eventually, physically and psychologically fatigued, he was sidelined. Initially this seemed like the end of the world to him; however, I encouraged him to exercise, and he had time to expand some of his interests. In the end it marked a new beginning for him. His health was restored, his family life improved and, ironically, due to the regionalisation of the business, his own power base grew while those in the centre continued to live on an increasingly sharpening knife edge.

Of course, if you work for yourself, either running a business or in a freelance capacity, the danger of putting in more hours than is healthy is equally great – perhaps even greater if your office is within your own home. Where and how are the lines then to be drawn between your working and your leisure hours? If your life isn't to become entirely taken over by what you do for a living you have to be very strict and recognise that, unless you consciously set up barriers of time and space between home and work, your life will become unbalanced.

I discussed this very problem with a friend of mine who was a freelance designer working from home. He found that closing the door to his home-based office was not enough, as it was like a magnet to him 24 hours a day. Eventually we came up with a solution. Fortunately, the office had a door into his garden so we locked the internal door (so that he could no longer wander in from the house), making a division that allowed him to create a physical barrier between work and home. Wherever it is you work, you have to ensure that you keep the commitment it requires in perspective.

On your death bed, will you regret not having spent more time in the office? Or will you instead want to be remembered for things you achieved in your personal life, such as bringing up your children, helping your community – or even being a good friend?

'There's no one else who can do my job – I'm totally indispensable.'

This is self-delusion. If you have ever left one company to go to another you will know exactly how replaceable you are. Even though you may seem to be doing a job better than you can imagine anyone else doing it, once you've gone the waters close over and, sorry to break it to you, you're history. Someone else could do your job – better, worse or simply in a different way, but the tasks would still be completed. Part of the package with this particular self-delusion is an inability to delegate ('I have to do it because otherwise it won't get done properly,' you say) and a reluctance to turn down extra tasks, thereby further expanding your workload. **Do you hoover up new responsibilities and have a reputation as just the man who can't say no?** You'll be the first one to cancel a social commitment because something needs finishing at the office, and it's unlikely that you'll use up your full holiday allowance ('I've got too much in my in-tray,' you'll bleat to your wife).

Putting in ridiculous hours because you think that no one can perform in the office as well as you is arrogant and, in the longer term, self-destructive – you will probably get exhausted through overwork, with the inevitable consequence that you will simply get worse at your job. What sort of a result is that? Setting acceptable and transparent expectations is one of the most important factors in generating sustainable or long-term partnerships. **The alignment of reasonable expectations between you/your employer/your client is the only way you can perform consistently and at your best – and avoid falling short of expectations**. You can only try so hard, work so hard and demand so much before there is a point of diminishing return. More then becomes less, especially for you. When you are buried right in the depths of this cycle, it's hard to be in the helicopter above it all and realise how self-defeating this way of working really is. The good new is this: it's tricky but not impossible to pull yourself out of it. It's in everyone's best interests (except the competition) for you to work more smartly and hit the target 100 per cent of the time.

The balanced wheel

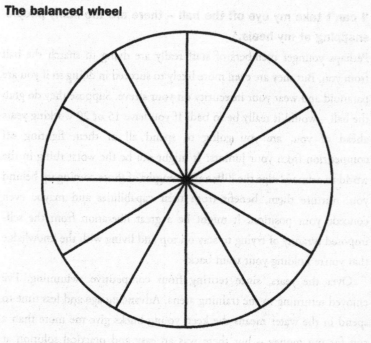

The buckled wheel

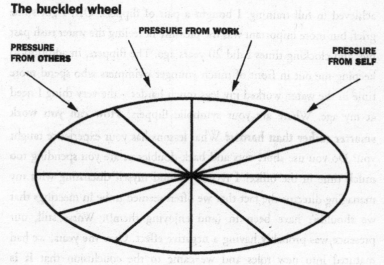

PRESSURE FROM WORK

PRESSURE
FROM OTHERS

PRESSURE
FROM SELF

'I can't take my eye off the ball – there are too many people snapping at my heels.'

Perhaps younger members of staff really are dying to snatch the ball from you. But they are even more likely to succeed in doing so if you are paranoid and wear your insecurity on your sleeve. Suppose they do grab the ball – would it really be so bad? If you have 15 or 20 working years ahead of you, are you going to spend all of them fighting off competition from your juniors? It might not be the worst thing in the world to acknowledge the different strengths of those coming up behind you, nurture them, benefit from their capabilities and maybe even concede your position. It might be a great liberation from the self-imposed tyranny of trying to stay on top and living with the knowledge that you're holding your team back.

Over the years, since retiring from competitive swimming, I've enjoyed returning to the training arena. Advancing age and less time to spend in the water means the keen young bucks give me more than a run for my money – but there was an easy and practical solution at hand, and one that made it possible for me to swim at the pace I'd achieved in full training. I bought a pair of flippers. OK, I got some grief, but more important was the pleasure of feeling the water rush past me, and clocking times I did 20 years ago. The flippers, in addition to keeping me out in front of much younger swimmers who spend more time in the water, worked my legs much harder – the very thing I need at my age. Where are your symbolic flippers? **How can you work smarter rather than harder?** What lessons has your experience taught you? Do you use short cuts and back-doubles or are you spending too much time in the office? I recently found myself discussing with my managing director the fact that we often seemed to be in meetings that we shouldn't have been in (and enjoying them!). Worse still, our presence was probably having a negative effect. Over the years, we had matured into new roles and we came to the conclusion that **it is** essential regularly to examine the tasks we perform against the role we are engaged in. All too typically there's a mismatch of which you might be totally unaware.

Some of the most effective and most professional people I have met are those who are always out of the office by 5.30 p.m. If you have a good team of trusted and conscientious individuals, you should be able to leave them working – they don't need you hovering over them. Similarly, if you are conscientious yourself you should have the confidence to leave the office when you are ready – and not simply be there to put on a show. And if you need to get some fresh air in the middle of the afternoon so that you can think more clearly (or perhaps want to take your lunch hour at 2.00 p.m. in order to go to the gym when it's less crowded) you should have the confidence to do so. Simply square it with your boss – or if you are the boss, tell your staff what you are up to and encourage them to do the same.

I was helping a top manager in an international company who was wrestling with the problem of getting enough exercise. I advised him to put it in his diary at lunchtime. If his secretary needed to bump it, she had to reschedule the work-out for that day. I asked him if he walked out of his office at 4.00 p.m. with a gym bag, what message he'd be giving his staff: a) that he was skiving off or b) that he trusted them to get on with things in his absence? He's now regularly seen leaving the office at 4.00 p.m. with his games kit slung over one shoulder.

'I prefer the office to home.'

It's unlikely that you'll admit this to yourself, let alone your family. It is perfectly possible, however, that the real, underlying reason for staying late at work is that you simply prefer being in the office to anywhere else – perhaps you've forgotten how to operate in any other environment. This is perhaps the most insidious and unhealthy reason for putting in excessive hours at the office. For many people the office is where they feel in most control. There are no children to answer back, no wife to challenge opinions and no list of DIY tasks to be completed. **In the corporate world you can be master of the universe, whereas at home you may feel that you are the lowest in the pecking order, one below the cat.** It's not much surprise then if you are tempted to linger in the office.

The journalist Katherine Whitehorn wrote: 'I yield to no-one in my admiration for the office as a social centre, but it's no place to get any work done.' How true that is – and on so many different levels. The workplace is often somewhere that people retreat to in order to hide from their other commitments, and in doing so they lose touch with the other parts of their life. A common consequence of this pattern of behaviour is that relationships in the office become more important than those at home, and **if someone is treating you like top cat in the office the temptation may be to jump in her lap.** How many men do you know who have had a fling in the office, with disastrous and long-term consequences for their families, not to mention themselves? I know too many.

There are plenty of dangers in lingering in the office for too many hours every day, apart from the cliché of waking up in bed next to your secretary (or, worse still, married to her). There is also the inevitable pattern of lost friendships. If you are constantly in the office and unavailable to see your friends, they will start to make the assumption that you are always working late and so will stop inviting you out. You then lose your friendships and, as a result, have nothing left in your life but work – and so the vicious circle completes itself.

The result of neglecting friends – and family too – is that if anything happens to your job, you'll find that there is no one there to support you when you most need it. It is a reflection of how unbalanced your life has become if you turn around and see an empty space – a void which you inevitably create when work expands into every area of your life.

Perhaps, on leaving university you were recruited into a job – possibly not the ideal one, but its shortcomings were made up for by the social opportunities and the drinks in the pub. Promotions came and were welcomed, but as you moved up the scale, the pub was no longer an appropriate place for you to be, and work started to become your focus. The arrival of children may have coincided with further promotion, and any problems in the office now fell on deaf ears at home. Your wife was too busy and tired from looking after the kids to listen, and any time you had to spend with friends had been eaten away by your other commitments – and indeed by theirs.

When you reach this point you may feel as though you are running on a treadmill, focusing on a dot on the wall put there by someone else and going at a pace which is being cranked up by someone else. You are running nowhere in a fog of exhaustion with just a dot to keep you on track. I assume we all want to be as far from this scenario as possible, and by working through what's important to you and setting goals accordingly, you should be able to avoid it. Aim for a 'dot on the wall' which is your dot, not someone else's. Peter, an extremely successful friend of mine with a well-balanced life, recently said to me: 'If I have to stay late in the office, then I feel I'm not properly organised.' He has never allowed himself to be drawn in by the macho business of being at his desk until the small hours. Anyone who does this has lost sight of what really matters and will have no time for the other areas in his life.

So what is balance?

Time spent in the different areas of your life is key to maintaining balance. To help visualise your time, picture your life as a bicycle wheel divided by its spokes. Each section represents a different activity or aspect of your life. There may be a certain amount of overlap and duplication between some areas, but, as a broad guide, you should aim to have this many departments in your life:

Family

Partner

Friends

Hobbies/Creative

Work

Fitness

Altruism

Sleep

Spiritual/Relaxation

Time off

Eating

Fun

Look at your own 'wheel': is there time allocated to each of these areas? Or are some of your sections empty? If your work, for example, has really taken over your life, the other sections will gradually have emptied themselves – Sleep and Relaxation will go first, then Altruism, probably followed by Fitness and Hobbies. Friends might cling on for a while but will eventually fall out of the circle – even Family and Partner could eventually be pushed out if they haven't already jumped out voluntarily. **You can't operate for 24 hours a day on one setting – if you do, you will work yourself into an unsustainable routine.**

Much of this book concerns what you believe in. Whether you are an atheist, a member of a faith, or something in between, what you cannot deny is that life is a unique opportunity and you might as well live it to the full. **Whether you think this life is all that you have or that it's part of some greater plan, you have to engage in what you *feel* matters in life – and fulfil it accordingly.**

The well-balanced wheel

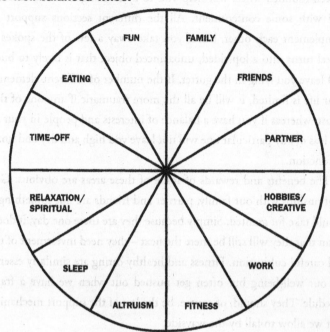

The workaholic's buckled wheel

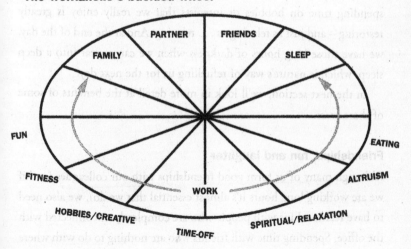

A well-rounded wheel will help you to cycle along the road smoothly and with some contentment. All the different sections support and complement each other, but if you take away a few of the spokes the wheel turns into a lop-sided, unbalanced object that is likely to buckle and leave you lying in the gutter. If the number of different elements in your life is limited, it will be all the more traumatic if any one of them is lost, whereas if you have a balance of interests and people in your life, the loss of any particular one will not leave you high and dry and unable to function.

The benefits and rewards of some of these areas are obvious. Good relationships with our family, partner and friends are not something we should take for granted. Simply because they are there one day, it doesn't mean that they will still be there the next – they need investment of time and careful cultivation. Fitness and healthy eating are similarly essential for our well-being but often get pushed out when we have a frantic schedule. They should, of course, be the last of the support mechanisms that we allow to fall by the wayside.

How we spend our leisure time (and zealously ensuring that we have plenty of it) is crucial to our zest and energy. Having fun and spending time on hobbies or interests that we really enjoy is greatly restoring – and just as relaxing as . . . relaxing. And at the end of the day, we have those long hours of darkness when we can retreat into a deep sleep, which is nature's way of refuelling us for the next day.

In the next section, we'll look in more detail at the benefits of some of these areas.

Friendships, fun and laughter

Although many of us form good friendships with our colleagues (and if we are working long hours it's almost essential that we do), we also need to have relationships with people who are completely unconnected with the office. Spending time with friends who are nothing to do with where we work is vital and helps to keep our wheel balanced.

Naturally we all have friends who rely on us for help and support, and we should always make time for them and be there when they need us. But we may also have friends who are negative and draining, and we should certainly be cautious about spending too much time with this group of people; they will continually erode our own mission to be more motivated and energised. The friends we should seek out and try to spend as much time with as possible are those who are positive, optimistic and fun to be with. These are the ones who can still make you feel good hours after you've left their company. If you don't already have friends like this, you should make it a goal to find some – believe me they exist, and their company is better than a bottle of Bollinger, giving you all the fizz but not the hangover. What is it that we gain from our most enjoyable and fun friendships? What is the single most enjoyable thing about being with people we like, apart from the simple, comforting sense of companionship? I believe it's the shared pleasure of laughter.

We all know instinctively, without being told by the experts, that laughter is good for us. When we laugh, there is a release of tension which can only be beneficial for our physical and mental well-being. Laughter is said to to boost the immune system, to have healing power and to aid recovery from illness. It can also help us to get rid of stored up emotions, pressure and problems. There's a wonderful and utterly simple saying about laughter, by a writer called Mary Pettibone Poole: 'He who laughs, lasts.' And apparently even that is true – laughter has been linked to longevity. Perhaps you think I'm cracking laughter up too much, but if you're sceptical it's worth looking at what happens to you physically when you laugh. After a few minutes:

● Your tear glands are stimulated, producing moisture which contains immunoglobulin, an antibody that defends against infection. The area that controls laughter is very close to the crying spot, which is why we often end up crying when we laugh and laughing when we cry.

- Your brain will produce endorphins, a natural, painkilling drug.
- Stress hormones produced by the adrenal glands are reduced.
- Blood pressure increases during laughter but drops below resting level afterwards.
- Muscles tense and relax – think of it as internal jogging.
- The supply of oxygen and blood to the tissues is increased.

It's no wonder then, when all these positive things are going on in our bodies, that having a good laugh is so much fun. The fact that it's actually doing us so much good should tell us not only that we should never suppress it but that we should positively seek it out. And if we can't find friends to share it with, we should sit down with our favourite comedy video and let Frasier, Frank Skinner, *Fawlty Towers*, or whatever pushes the right button, help us get helpless with laughter.

I learned the importance of trying to see the funny side of certain situations all those years ago when I lost my hair. I had, since going bald, found cycling a little hazardous, especially during the summer. Let's face it, I could hardly wear a visor or goggles on a bicycle – I could just imagine the taunts: 'Hey Biggles!' – so I just had to put up with temporary blindness. My lack of eyebrows was slightly inconvenient, as they are designed to prevent perspiration from dripping into your eyes. On the squash court or rugby pitch, for example, the salty sweat would half blind me. Somehow swimming was much safer. When my hair first fell out, the skin on my head was tender and it was decided that I should protect it. I wore a thick lady's rubber swimming cap plus a scrum cap, causing a certain amount of ridicule from my team-mates. Thank goodness they didn't realise that the hair had fallen out of my nostrils. If they had, they might have bought me a nose clip, and I would have looked like the famous synchronized swimmer Esther Williams, though not quite so pretty.

One day, my father took me to London to buy a wig. We ended up going for a blonde one so that my lack of eyebrows wouldn't be so noticeable. The next problem was the lack of sideburns and, although Dad didn't approve of this solution, I solved it by getting a longer wig. Dad wore his hair short and slicked back with Brylcreem to keep it in place. Millfield had rules about how long hair should be and the wig broke them all, so I knew I was going to have some fun with it. The first time I was reported to the prefects, one of them ordered me to get my hair cut. In an instant I had my wig off. 'Is this short enough?' I asked. There were roars of laughter from the other prefects. My main concern about having a wig was the cost. Every time one of my four brothers had a haircut I claimed my haircutting allowance. This was particularly lucrative since I had so many brothers. I also fined my mother every time I caught her buying haircare products.

There have been other perks of being bald. I was once interviewed on television by Selina Scott, who was fascinated by my hairlessness. She demanded proof that I really didn't have a hair on my body so I rolled up my trouser leg for her to have a feel. To my amazement (and that of everyone else in the studio) she then told me to take my trousers off! Everyone roared with laughter and needless to say I declined the invitation. Having a sense of humour has always helped me survive the tricky times and laughing either by myself or with others has been key to my well-being. **Humour is not optional. Humour is what makes us human**.

Altruism

If you never look outwards you will never see your own life in perspective. Frantic with work, busy with your family and preoccupied with your own health, you could end up seeing things through the wrong end of the telescope. Do you picture yourself at the very centre of the universe or as a small part of the much greater whole? You are, of course, the latter. It is vital to remind yourself regularly how you fit into the wider picture and to make sure that you don't lose track of how privileged you really are. Make connections with people who are part of a very different sphere from yourself, put your feet on the ground and get your hands dirty.

In Douglas Adam's *Hitch Hiker's Guide to the Galaxy*, Zaphod Beeblebrox, President of the Universe, is put into a vortex that gives him the 'exactly what we don't want' perspective, i.e. the perspective showing how very insignificant we are in relation to the universe. Astronauts have often been very forcibly struck by this, especially those who stood on the moon and looked back at the earth. I once heard Mrs John Glenn say 'when my husband got back from the moon' as though he had just popped out to the corner shop and come home again. How else could she cope with it? We all have a limited perspective and sometimes that's a good thing.

What we need when it comes to our failings, problems and successes, however, is a sense of proportion as much as one of perspective. Throughout this book, we have been looking at turning failure and problems into aspirations and achievements. Achievement, however, can equally be a problem in its own right. I've watched people struggle with it, and it is something that has to be managed. As we move up the corporate ladder we become more powerful. We're all familiar with the saying that power tends to corrupt while absolute power corrupts absolutely, but are we aware of its dangers in our own lives? As we achieve more we become more important and often increasingly ambitious, and our opinions become more valued. Our voice becomes louder until it threatens to deafen us to others, and we begin to believe our own press. Status in life is seductive, addictive and destructive – and can leave us entirely without a sense of proportion.

How long can you live with your head in the ether without becoming high on it? The sane and well-balanced among successful people get their hands dirty. They get themselves involved with people's problems in the community, and although they would see their actions as altruistic, they are also helping themselves. In making contact with the broader issues of life, they keep their feet on the ground, put their own difficulties in perspective and maintain a sense of proportion. **We should all make time for altruistic activity, not least because it reminds us where we fit into the world.**

Relaxation and me-time

As well as time with family, friends and colleagues, you need time exclusively with yourself. Call it what you like: 'me-time', 'time out' or 'self-time', this is time when you have to be selfish. It need be no longer than five or ten minutes, but if necessary it must be put in your diary and protected from all other commitments and demands. **Make time for listening to your own voice, and for exploring what you feel about the things you have been doing and the new things you have learnt in your life – not just in the work context.** It's not just the doing and the learning but the exploring which can create a sense of forward momentum and energy.

It can be a time to examine your battle scars, some of which will be emotional ones. As we mentioned in the Introduction, the ups and downs are what create interest in your personal landscape. Bill Mitchell, a leading clinical psychiatrist who is a friend of mine says: 'You have to look around and see the view of where you've come from.' Only by giving yourself time to do this will you appreciate your own achievement and take stock of the pool of knowledge, skills and experience that you have built up. By exploring this and gauging your own response you will be in a better position to make changes to your life and how you live it.

This is quite literally time for recreation at a very basic level, a window in which you 're-create' yourself and rediscover aspects of yourself which are easily submerged or eroded by the sheer weight of all the commitments you have to fulfil – family, friends, career. So what do you do with your recreation time? You do pretty much anything you like, as long as its legal and helps you regain your sense of self.

It could be something as simple as reading a book purely for pleasure, listening to some music, looking at some pictures in a gallery – or even painting one yourself. I find painting a good way to relax and tend to take my paints on holiday – though I know I'll probably get teased about it. Last summer I was sitting on the beach with friends, about to start a picture, and held up a pencil to measure the perspective. Colin, a balloonist friend who has broken many world records and is poised to fly a balloon to the edge of space, quipped wittily: 'It's an HB7 – I can see it from here!' From then on I was given the nickname 'Van Dunc'. I am not a particularly good artist, but painting makes me feel good so I have learned to take the teasing. **You should never allow others' opinions of your ability (or lack of it!) to deter you from something you enjoy or find fulfilling – and definitely never let it prevent you from doing it**. Even the light-hearted ribbing that your friends might subject you to could be enough to put you off – but keep in your mind that you are not doing it for them, you are doing it for **you**. Perhaps you used to enjoy painting yourself and still have some watercolours sitting in the attic – why not get them out and rediscover an old pleasure? You might prefer something more physical like going for a long walk (and making sure you stop to admire the view). Or it could be something more specifically structured to help you relax, like yoga or T'ai chi, a system of controlled body movements which has been described as 'meditation in movement'.

The primary objective for this segment of your life is to take yourself away from pressurised situations, to be on your own, to enjoy solitude and to gain strength from it, whether you are sitting at an easel, walking the dog, or lying on the floor slowly breathing in and out while listening to an old Pink Floyd album. This is time for you.

Breathing – an aid to relaxation

Some of us find it hard to relax – it should come naturally but if we are wound up and pressurised much of the time it's hardly surprising that it's sometimes difficult for our bodies and minds to slip into cruising gear when we're usually grinding uphill in first.

Certain breathing techniques can slow us down for a moment and induce a wonderful state of calm. This is very helpful if you are someone whose shoulders are usually up around your ears. First of all, notice how you breathe when you're feeling anxious (fast and shallow) and then learn to do the opposite to achieve the desired result. Without pressing, rest your hands on the area between your rib cage and your navel. As you inhale, you should feel your hands lifting slightly upwards and outwards, with the upper chest inflating last. Hold your breath for a second and then exhale, making sure that you are emptying your lungs from the top and finishing when your hands have moved back to their original position. If this makes you feel light-headed you should stop and breathe normally for a while. This technique is useful not just for helping you to relax, but also in situations where you are feeling tense and panicky.

Controlled breathing saved me during my baptism by fire in the public speaking arena. At the age of 23, fresh out of the water, IBM asked me to address some of their managers during a training seminar, and in due course I had an audience of 12 of them peering at me and listening politely. Although it was challenging, I already had extensive experience of speaking to swimming audiences and knew my speech had been well received when I was asked back to speak again. This time, however, they wanted a rehearsal. The night before the event, a stretch limo arrived to take me to Wembley Arena. I went through security and into the auditorium, where four men were sitting in the front row. One leaned forward and said, in an American accent, 'Thanks for coming here tonight, Duncan. Let's hear what you're going to say tomorrow.' So, all miked up and feeling very strange, I spoke to just four of them in that vast, dark and echoing space. On finishing, there was a single hand clap and the one who had spoken to me at the beginning lent forward in his seat and said, 'Thank you Duncan. Before you go, let me say this: we are the bosses of the four companies that make up IBM. Tomorrow we are going to amalgamate the four companies and fire the 1700 staff attending. We will then rehire them. And let me tell you, IBM has a turnover the size of the French gross national product. We don't want any fuck-ups tomorrow.'

The following day arrived and I woke feeling sick to the pit of my stomach. The venue was huge, the client terrifying and, worse still, my fellow speaker, a very well-known actor and comedian, was a bag of nerves. He'd always made me laugh on television, but that day he was not fun or funny to be around. To this day, I have never witnessed anyone who has come even close to the stage fright he suffered from before that event. He roamed around backstage, panting, sweating profusely and trembling like a leaf. His condition was contagious. We both had to go on stage in front of 1700 dark suits, 1700 pairs of eyes. The breath control I had learned in the Olympic Arena paid dividends and I managed to speak without betraying even a hint of my inner fear. On stage my fellow speaker was fine too, of course. IBM has invited me back on a number of occasions and I'm very grateful for the launch platform they gave me for public speaking. I'm also grateful for that simple technique for controlling the sense of panic that sweeps over you in such situations.

Time off

Most working people now have somewhere between four and six weeks' paid holiday a year, but lots of us don't take it. We make any number excuses ranging from a heavy workload and a shortage of people to cover for us in our absence to clients insisting on our availability. None of these reasons is good enough to get in the way of you taking time out of your usual routine. **Time spent away from day-to-day work is essential if you want to restore your energy and vitality and regain the sense that you are not defined only by your job.** You can use this time to develop your relationship with your family and friends in a way that is impossible in the usual run of things. It is just as important to have time away from an exciting and unpredictable job as it is to have time away from a humdrum existence on the production line. But how difficult some men find it!

Picture this: a glorious sandy beach somewhere in southern Europe, children frolic in the waves, a woman lies on a sun-lounger reading *Captain Corelli's Mandolin*. A slightly balding, slightly pink man in stripy swimming trunks (brand new, you can tell by the crease) waddles awkwardly across the sand and perches next to his wife on the sun-bed. She looks up from her book. 'Where have you been, darling?' she asks. 'Just checking my emails,' he replies. Held tightly in his hand is his mobile phone, the grown-up's security blanket, and at exactly that moment it rings. 'Yup, yup, okay . . . right, yup, I'll get back to you in ten minutes,' he barks. 'Sorry darling,' he says, 'Crisis in the office. They're just sending a fax through to the hotel. Better go and deal with it. Won't be long.' So off he goes to reception and if you looked carefully you might almost imagine there was a spring in his step.

Do you recognise that man? We've all seen him, know him or, worst of all, are him. Is it you? Or is it someone you'd hate to become? What a sorry figure he is. Ill at ease in the holiday situation, attached by his umbilical telecommunications cord to his office and scarcely able to conceal his enthusiasm when he is offered a reprieve and can escape from the beach. If you identify in any way with this character, throw away your phone, book yourself a holiday, don't tell your secretary where you're going and relearn how to enjoy the sensation of sand between your toes.

Sleep

The last, but by no means the least, important thing you do in a day is sleep. But of all the elements that make up your life this is one which could make the biggest impact on the energy you have to put into your waking hours. However many hours you feel you need to put in at the office, however many hours you need to spend with your friends and family, you should fiercely protect your sleeping time. **Treat sleep as an investment – for every hour you spend in blissful slumber, you'll perform that much better during the day**.

Depriving a victim of sleep is a tried and tested form of torture successfully used by interrogators down the ages. Even under normal circumstances lack of sleep (often self-inflicted) can have dire consequences for our health and well-being – and conversely, being able to sleep well can have a hugely beneficial effect on our performance and energy. Given how important sleep is, it always amazes me how much people will spend on a car (literally tens of thousands of pounds) which they may not drive for more than an hour a day, while they resent paying even a few hundred pounds for a good mattress. Given that we probably spend at least seven or eight times as many hours in bed as at the wheel, this is ludicrous. It's really worth considering when you next buy a bed how much a good night's sleep can contribute to your general health and whether your expenditure on it reflects that.

Quantity and quality

The amount of sleep we need varies from individual to individual, but for most of us it's somewhere between seven and nine hours a night. If we are getting less than this over an extended period of time, we start to feel run down, and even if we just have a string of late nights over a short period we will suffer some mild effects. Similarly we can feel the benefits when we have had just the right amount of sleep – rather than hiding under the duvet groaning, we feel full of get-up-and-go when the alarm clock goes off in the morning. What happens when we're sleeping to give us that great feeling? Sleep is divided into different stages:

Stage 1: The dozing stage, when you might experience leg jerks and the sensation of stumbling or falling as you drift off to sleep

Stage 2: A series of sleeping cycles each lasting about 90 minutes and each progressively deeper, including some . . .

Stage 3: Very deep and restful sleep, known as 'slow wave sleep'

Stage 4: REM (rapid eye movement) – the phase in which you dream

Sleep which corresponds to this formula, i.e. good quality, uninterrupted, regular sleep is essential for:

● energy and vitality

● giving our organs a chance to rest

● allowing our immune system to recharge

● giving our subconscious an opportunity to release emotions and play out the day's events

Why you might be sleepless

There are lots of reasons why we may be getting less sleep than we really need, ranging from severe insomnia, for which we should seek the advice of a doctor, to stress, overwork and not being able to wind down. **You may be lying there wired, adrenalin coursing through your system, with zero chance of drifting into restorative sleep**. If you are having trouble sleeping, you should ask yourself why so that you can address the problem. Any of the following might be the causes of inadequate or broken sleep, and most of them can be addressed once recognised:

● stress and anxiety

● depression

- overwork
- illness and/or pain
- eating too heavily too late in the evening
- too much late night coffee, alcohol or cigarettes
- your mind being tired but your body still having energy (or perhaps vice versa)
- exercising too close to bedtime
- urinary problems
- noise (or even quiet if you are used to noise!)
- jet lag

The consequences of sleeplessness

There was a particular period in my life when sleep was squeezed out. It nearly cost me my health and it certainly cost me my short-term sanity. It was when I was studying for my degree in Business Management in the US and, along with the rest of the North Carolina swimming team, I was training for the 1976 Olympics over the Christmas holidays. Nothing I had ever done in or out of the water had prepared me for the extreme nature of what we did in that fortnight. There was no land training, but we swam twice a day until our arms felt like lead drainpipes – covering a distance of 20,000 metres a day (400 lengths of a 50-metre pool, or 800 lengths of the average local swimming pool). We would go back to the hotel (where six of us were crammed into one room) and collapse. As my body became more and more physically broken down I found myself too tired to sleep. Night after night I lay in a state of no man's land between sleep and consciousness, interrupted by the occasional muscle spasm. The tiredness made me bad tempered, and since the only person I could blame was my coach, the confrontations between us became increasingly vocal.

On my return to college after Christmas things didn't get better. My grades were horrific, and I had to have a private tutor to help me out.

We all had trouble staying awake in lectures because of our fatigue from swimming, in addition to which the pressure of academic work meant that we rarely got to bed before midnight. Studying late for exams was not seen as a good enough excuse to miss early morning training sessions, and as time wore on I became totally exhausted and started to under-perform on all fronts.

I was suffering from a classic case of sleep deprivation, which causes stress, over-tiredness, irritability and anxiety. One thing I didn't suffer from (and I think I was lucky) was recurrent infection (a good night's sleep plays a key role in helping prevent illness). If this is not enough to make you recognise the importance of adequate sleep, contemplate this: **sleep aids the replenishment of hormones such as testosterone, crucial to a man's sense of well-being and ability to reproduce.** Although the latter did not bother me at all at that time, it could be very significant for anyone attempting to have children – or to have fun. Do remember, while we're on the subject, that exercising late at night can also prevent full, restful sleep.

How to seek sleep

As well as psychological tricks to induce sleep, (counting sheep or writing your worries down on a piece of paper before going to bed and leaving it outside the bedroom are just two of them) there are plenty of practical methods of inducing sleep. Before you go to bed:

- Play relaxing music.
- Drink herbal tea or a milky drink.
- Have a hot bath with a relaxing infusion such as lavender.
- Make sure your bedroom is dark, quiet and not too hot (a cool room will assist you to a deeper, more restorative sleep).
- Make sure that anything you eat within a few hours of bed-time is sleep-inducing. Foods containing magnesium, calcium and vitamin B6 all have a tranquilising effect. Try bananas and nuts.

- Try to avoid sleeping pills, some of which have a sedative effect that lasts throughout the day, making you feel drowsy just when you need to be performing at your best. There are, however, many natural remedies, which have a less extreme effect on your system. Any trained health food shop assistant will be able to advise you which to try.

Although millions of people seek advice every year for problems with sleep, there is no magic cure. For many sufferers, the cause is a lack of balance: too much work, too much anxiety, a discrepancy between how much the body and mind are being exercised, even too little fresh air. Sleep will always feature in your wheel, but the quality of the sleep you get will be dependent on how well-balanced you keep the other elements between the spokes.

What kind of pool do you want to swim in? A murky one? Or one where all the muck and debris which cloud the water have been filtered out? If you swim in a clean pool and put on your goggles as well, you will be able to see where you are going. You'll then be able to swim towards your goals without colliding with another swimmer. Your wave-breakers (lane ropes) are vital here too — they dissipate the turbulence from neighbouring lanes and help you swim straight and in calm waters undistracted by anything going on around you.

Action

- Review your responses to Chapter 3's action points.
- If you have not already done so, draw up your own circle and divide it with spokes. Fill in all the domains currently in your life (including sleep) and the ones you wish to introduce into your life.

- Turn back to your swimming lanes and explore what filters you could use to clear the debris in each of them – these are the unproductive distractions which might be getting between you and your goals.

- Examine all the activities in the segments of your circle and ask yourself if there are any that are taking up too much time – with counter-productive results. Time in the office could well be one of these and could be giving diminishing returns. Sleep is unlikely to be taking up too much time – it's probably already being squeezed.

- Are there any significant areas of your life where you feel you have two shallow ends? Aim to rectify this.

- Think smart about how you spend your time – can you take care of two activities simultaneously? Take friends to a comedy show? Have an adventurous holiday with the family? It may take a bit of organisation – but it will be time well spent since you will be maximising your opportunities and killing several birds with one stone. Time is at a premium, don't waste it. Make at least three arrangements in the next fortnight.

- Look at the elements in your circle and write the time you think you should be spending on each activity in your swimming lanes.

CHAPTER 5

SWIMMING AGAINST THE TIDE –

Step Five:
Learn from your Failings

A worst day, an off day, a bad hair day – we all have them, even baldies like me. These are the days when things aren't going right for you and you can't quite put your finger on the reason why.

A worst day is when you feel pessimistic and incapable of achieving your goals. You spend far too much time in wishful thinking and the words 'if only' and 'supposing I had' are endlessly on your lips. When you look in the mirror all you see is a receding hairline, a double chin and ample evidence of the victory of the forces of gravity as everything gets pulled inexorably downwards – including your spirit. A worst day is like a grey Monday morning: your body feels like lead and your brain like porridge. These are days when life gets on top of you, and although you've done everything in your power to make it all work, things still seem to be out of your control. **On worst days negative voices in your head taunt you with what you haven't achieved rather than reminding you of what you have, and getting out of bed seems to require more effort than scaling the Matterhorn.** A worst day is when nothing you do seems good enough: you're not successful, intelligent, thoughtful or good-looking enough, and you don't feel that you are performing well in your roles as husband, father or friend. This, as you would recognise on a good day, is a self-destructive thought pattern that can only result in further negative thinking. But on your worst days you aren't necessarily rational and, even if it's all purely in your imagination, these feelings are very real, creating self-doubt and erosion of confidence. Worst days do happen when you're young, but somehow they seem to occur more regularly as you trundle into that murky and unwelcoming territory called middle age.

But enough of all this depressing stuff. Is there something you can do to influence your own attitudes and reactions when life seems more of an uphill struggle than usual? **Is there a way of creating consistency in your moods and in your ability to be positive when things are going wrong?** Should you motivate yourself to go running when you can hardly be bothered to get out of bed? The answer, of course, is yes.

Your armour against a worst day

There are plenty of steps you can take to shift yourself into a more positive pattern of thinking – and I have talked about most of them in previous chapters. It's when the going gets tough that the time and the commitment you have given to these areas of your life will really pay off.

This is the ammunition in your arsenal to deploy against worst days (or even worst weeks or worst months):

- Look after your diet, health and fitness.
- Assess whether you are doing a job which sufficiently fulfils you intellectually, morally and financially.
- Ensure you give time to your relationships with family and friends.
- Spend time on hobbies and interests outside work.
- Maintain a sense of humour – and a sense of proportion.
- Have a 'support team' who push you on when you are feeling demoralised.

If you have invested in all these things, you will have some armour against the negative and pessimistic feelings that can drag you down on your worst days. They are part of your strategy for holding on to your self-confidence, the loss of which is one of the most likely outcomes from days like these. A 'worst day' is a psychological state – a grey Monday morning inside your head. You need to open the curtains and see what's outside – you might find it's a sunny Friday afternoon. Overcoming that bad-hair-day feeling can be like coming up to the surface to find brilliant sunshine after swimming in the murky depths.

Ritual and routine are essential reinforcements to all the ammunition above. There's a saying that when the going gets tough, the tough get going. **One way of making yourself keep going when you seem to be swimming against the tide is to have a fairly rigid routine which you simply never deviate from**. It may feel like drudgery at the time, but the importance of having a structure to your life is never more important than when things around you are hard going.

Your commitment to fitness is vital whether or not you actually feel like taking any exercise. If, for example, you always get up and jog on

Tuesday and Thursday mornings or meet friends to play badminton on Saturday morning, the very last thing you should do if you are under pressure or feel time is too precious is to give up on these arrangements. Research has proved that regular exercise can be enough to keep away symptoms of depression. This is due to the release of feel-good hormones, such as endorphins and serotonin, which your body produces during physical activity. If this isn't incentive enough to keep you from slumping in an armchair, then remember that exercise can also help to make you feel you are in control. Indeed, it's one of the best ways of turning a worst day into a better one.

The same principle applies to all the other activities outlined in the last chapter that give you time for personal fulfilment. Whether it's Italian on Wednesday evenings, walking the dog on Sunday mornings or going for a regular stress-relieving massage, the worst time to let any of these disciplines go by the board is when you are under pressure. It's precisely when you feel negative that you most need a framework to your life.

As a swimmer, I held on to my belief that I could win an Olympic gold medal (even when my times were telling me it wasn't possible) partly with the help of routine and ritual. The routine of training was even more essential when I found it painful to get out of bed, and the ritual of undressing in a very particular way for competition became more important than ever as an aid to concentration.

Hitting rock bottom

One of the most common causes of 'worst days' is simple exhaustion. When you are tired you are vulnerable to just about everything – your temper is short, your tolerance of other people is low and your immune system is fragile. During my time in North Carolina I was very close to the edge of my physical and psychological tolerance, but the day I hit absolute rock bottom was also a turning point and gave me a new appreciation of my priorities. Sometimes I think this has to happen and that you only start to build and grow after you've been right down as far as you think it's possible to go. Perhaps it's rather like swimming: it's easy to push yourself up to the surface once you've connected with the very bottom of the pool.

On one particular day I had an accountancy exam in the morning, and the homework I had been set had not gone well. I had struggled with the double entry system and the two figures had not balanced as they should have. I spent an hour performing a reconciliation on the numbers to no avail, and the later it got the more tired I became and the more mistakes I made. I finally succeeded in balancing the accounts just before 4.30 a.m. and crawled into bed exhausted. The alarm woke me from a deep sleep at 5.55 a.m. I was conditioned to sit up in bed and then spring to my feet, having learned from experience that if my feet did not hit the floor while the alarm was still going I would just sink back into sleep. Even the simple task of dressing was difficult that day, and the warm-up for the work-out drained me.

'I've seen enough of you. Why don't you go down to the deep end where you'll be out of my sight,' roared the coach. This was the last straw, and as I stood up in the water profanities started to pour out of me and I hurled my kickboard towards him, narrowly missing his head. With that, his temper snapped and he began to rant and rave. I ignored him. I was going home – to England.

A few hours later I felt strong enough to face my coach again. I walked up the three flights of stairs to his office, too tired now to be angry. He sat silhouetted against the window. 'I'm going home,' I declared. There was a long silence before he spoke, and when he did it was in a tone I had never heard him use before. No fronts, no jokes, no double meanings. 'Duncan, before you leave I'd just like to say one thing. If I don't work you as hard as I possibly can then I am cheating you.' This sudden change of mood put me off my guard, and, before I knew it, I was sitting down discussing the future with this man in a way

I had never done with anyone before. He would not expel me, but if he allowed that morning's confrontation to go unpunished, then his position of authority with the rest of the swimming team would be compromised. He couldn't punish me by working me any harder. I was at breaking point already.

This was the day I recognised that the coach was my champion – someone who completely believed I could achieve my goals. After practice that afternoon, I had time to reflect on what had happened that day and realised that I had spent most of my life fighting the people trying to help me. I also realised that if I was sent home then I would be saying goodbye to my Olympic dream and all it meant to me. At last, I recognised Don Easterling as a friend and co-conspirator in my dream, which made training much more palatable. After the confrontation, I felt a new strength in the knowledge that I was no longer a lone crusader but it had taken an outburst like that to get me moving forwards again. The episode showed me that **we all need someone who can tip the scales in our favour by being positive and telling us, 'You can do it.'**

Failing – in order to succeed

Success of any significance is not easily achieved – it is usually gained through a combination of hard work and tenacity. If this sounds like a lot of effort, it's meant to. Any success worth having is worth working for, and if it comes without you quite realising how, it can be hard to sustain and almost impossible to repeat. Perhaps this is most apparent in sport. I have watched athletes being catapulted to extraordinary levels of achievement and fame at a very young age, but soon afterwards they are confronted by a crisis of confidence and go into freefall. The slide starts because they have no real knowledge of how and what they did to achieve their own historic performance, they have no way of putting a stop to their plummeting performance and they are remembered as just a flash in the pan.

One such athlete was Gerald Mörken, a German swimmer. I still have recurring nightmares about this man's feet. Having dragged myself out of a long series of 'worst days', I was finally swimming well again when I was confronted in the final of the European Championships with the soles of Mörken's feet disappearing in front of me during his world-record-shattering swim. The poor chap never really recovered. He clawed his way back over a period of years to final in some major events, but never really saw the same record-breaking form again – or the fulfilment of his indisputable physical potential. It had happened too quickly, perhaps too effortlessly, for him and he couldn't repeat his success.

When you are feeling negative, think of this (appropriately negative) definition of success – it might even make you feel closer to achieving it:

Success is the defeat of failure.

This never has more resonance than when you come across someone who appears to have been handed the worst that life has to offer but through strength of character and refusal to be beaten comes out on top. These are the people who survive and win in spite of physical disability, personal tragedy and a seemingly insurmountable mountain of obstacles and misfortune. Whether it's conscious or entirely natural to them, they demonstrate a form of success that is, in effect, a stubborn refusal to accept failure.

I learnt a lot from a boy at my school called Lewis. He had had polio, which had left him with a club foot and a hooked arm, and he also suffered from stunted growth. None of this, at least on the face of it, appeared to affect him, and everyone seemed to respect him. He was probably one of the most courageous people I have ever met. During a period when I was wallowing in a sea of self-pity over my baldness, an encounter with this particular boy made me see that I mustn't let it get the better of me – my adversity had to be put into context and shrugged off.

One day, as I walked into the room, he looked up at me and, for a fraction of a second, a knowing smile touched his lips. 'What's your problem, Dunc?' he asked. His question sank into my soul. I realised that I had created my own misery. It was up to me to make the most of my life. I had been lucky that I hadn't broken my neck and become paralysed when I had fallen from the tree. Considering what might have happened, I was pretty lucky to get away with just losing my hair – which has subsequently saved me a great deal of time counting hairs left behind in the bath. I also realised that it was perhaps more than coincidence that I had lost my hair and seemed to have a talent for swimming – they certainly seemed to go hand in hand. At all the big swimming meets, the swimmers had to shave their body hair off to become more streamlined – except me of course. It had taken years but at last I had come to terms with losing my hair. If someone had a problem with my bald head, I realised, then they were short-sighted and narrow-minded and certainly not worth the time of day. As the saying goes, 'Adversity makes or breaks you', and although I had had a close encounter I was now free from the shackles of self-pity and could go out and really enjoy myself. Although I would love to have had a head of thick glossy hair, I learned to live with my baldness, recognising that it offered some big advantages in the swimming pool – and a distinct point of difference on dry land.

Being aware of the difficulties that other people cope with on a daily basis is often enough to snap you out of a period of self-indulgence and self-pity. **You have to make the most of what you are given and conquer the difficulties; to do anything else is simply cowardly and self-indulgent.** For a long time I have realised that my baldness and my dyslexia were not just to be tolerated; they were conditions which drove me to find other meanings in life.

Being systematic about beating failure

Achieving certain goals will probably require a very systematic approach to eliminating the problems and shortcomings in your way. This will require a huge effort – which on your 'worst days' will seem particularly hard and often demoralising. After my first Olympics I had to go right back to basics with my swimming. Between the rigours of a love affair and a low carbohydrate diet, something went badly wrong. Whatever it was, the consequences left me reeling. It was as if my talent had been washed away, and with every swim my times got slower. The pendulum of confidence that had taken me nearly to the top a year before had swung back on its return trip, and there seemed to be no stopping it. It was as if all my new-found hopes for the future had drained away and I was going to be another Gerald Mörken.

The NCAAs – the big inter-university athletics championships in America – were a disaster. I didn't even reach the final. My coach had been bothered by the slight nod of my head to the right as I started each stroke, and when he filmed me underwater it appeared that my right hand lagged so far behind my left that it was literally acting as a brake, almost neutralising my pull. It turned out that I had a huge imbalance of strength and endurance between my right and left legs. This was the answer to the puzzle. There was nothing for it but to start again. I literally had to learn how to swim breaststroke from scratch, I came home in May depressed and dejected but on the mend. I had learned a great deal about my sport and myself, as you often do when you're at rock bottom and looking up.

I tackled the task of improving my times in a methodical and practical way, breaking down all the different stages and elements and discovering that in each area there was room for improvement, no matter how marginal. This methodical approach gives each element its own track record for you to call upon when faced with intense pressure. For me, this was Olympic Games and the relentless and probing self-doubt I so often experienced. When undressing before a race, I went through a specific routine, linking each physical action with a thought. I made sure that I kept warm for as long as possible, and this created a new ritual which was essential in helping me concentrate and conserve energy before the starting pistol was fired.

I worked on every last detail of my diving technique, as I knew that an improvement in this area could gain me a stroke. Putting my thumbs on the block gave me more control, prevented me from doing false starts and helped me push away from the blocks with my hands, meaning that I was faster to get away. I also spent months working on perfecting the pike dive, which gave me more height before I descended into the water. After months of working on this, I discovered a new kick which propelled me an extra 0.5 of a metre. By the time the 1980 Olympics came around, one of the Russian coaches said that although I was the slowest breaststroker among the top swimmers in the pool, I had the best dive and the best turn – so my concentration on this area had really paid off.

One of my problems was that I was not as big as the other breast-strokers and I lacked strength, so I invested an enormous amount of time in working with weights in order to build myself up. The extra strength gave me scope to work on the 'snap' that comes at the end of the kick.

The end result of breaking down all the elements was a marked improvement in my timings, but as the 1980 Olympics approached, a whole new set of difficulties started to get in the way. This was when I recognised that **it's more important to work hard when it hurts than when it all comes easily**. Of course there are times when pain is telling you to stop, but at other times you may need to work through your pain barrier to get out the other side.

Working hardest on your worst days

On your worst days you may need to focus your efforts more intensively than normal, working through your pain barrier to increase your strength, stamina and competitive edge. You might find this easier to achieve if, on some of your 'best days', you conserve your strength. Having held back some of your resources you will have a little in reserve for the days when you need that bit extra. The technique we used for this during the final stage of my Olympic 'journey' was known as 'tapering'. The 'taper' we worked on with team coach David Haller took place over a number of weeks and involved reducing the number of metres swum each day, but increasing the quality of the distances. By doing this we began to recover from the near exhaustion of full training and would experience a sensation not dissimilar to jet lag as our bodies struggled to adapt to the change. As exhaustion began to slip away, performance would rise and we began to feel invincible. Our times would improve and we would become addicted to the stopwatch. 'Save it,' the coach would shout at us. 'Back to the changing room!' **There is huge power in the notion of keeping something back, of conserving your grit**. This principle will help you fill up your reservoir so that on the days when your strength and stamina seem to be lacking you will have a supply to draw on.

If you don't pull out the stops on your worst days, your performance will fluctuate and look like this:

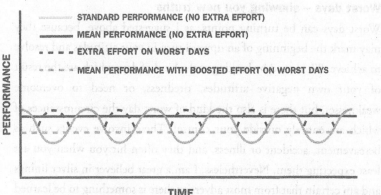

TIME

Given that you don't always pick the days on which you are obliged to turn in a good performance, the chances are that they will fall on your 'worst days'. You can't afford to have bad days. I certainly couldn't on the day of the Olympic final. I had to be at my peak on a certain day, in a certain place, and neither one was of my own choosing. If you work hard on your worst days, your mean performance will improve and you will create a new consistency for yourself. This is how your performance will then look:

When your performance reaches a certain level of consistency, then you have won before you even enter the water:

- You have a bad day
- So you call on your unspent reserves
- So you break through your negativity
- So you climb new heights
- So your performance becomes more consistently high
- So you learn to trust yourself and your ability
- So others trust you and your ability
- So the competition sees that you have few weaknesses
- So they respect you – and avoid you
- So you win

Worst days – showing you new truths

Worst days can be turning points, as I suggested above, because they may mark the beginning of an upward turn in your attitudes and resolve to achieve. We started by looking at the kind of days which are the result of your own negative attitudes, tiredness, or need to overcome weaknesses, but there is also the kind of worst day the circumstances of which are entirely outside your control. These involve events such as bereavement, accident or illness, and they often hit you when you are least expecting them. Nevertheless, I am a great believer in silver linings and am certain that from most adversity there is something to be learned or gained if we can distance ourselves enough to see the broader picture.

Following the accident that caused the loss of my hair, the next really terrible event of my life was the sudden death of my father when I was 15 years old. I remember with incredible clarity being called into the head's office at Millfield. It was puzzling. I could think of nothing I had done wrong. The head cleared his throat and fidgeted, which was out of character for him. 'I have some bad news Duncan,' he said, pausing. 'Your father is dead.' From that moment my life changed. I can't remember what he said to me after those shattering words. My father had needed to say so little, but everything he had said meant so much to me. Now he was gone. I found myself in the 'bolts', a hut where students could go in their spare time, and felt waves of emotion welling up inside me until they were so great they broke to the surface. I wept like a child, but as quickly as grief had come over me it subsided. I looked out of the window and saw the grass, the trees and the hedgerows, with the first signs of spring showing through, and was suddenly aware of the immense beauty of nature – and of life. At the same time I was nearly swept away by the thought of how short life is and how precious.

John, my eldest brother, came to pick me up for my father's funeral. I had never realised my father had so many friends. The crematorium was packed and there were mountains of flowers. His death had been due to a stroke at the age of 57, just one year after his mother had died of the same thing. It was an enormous shock to us all, especially my mother, who had four boys to look after. I felt guilty. Everyone looked so gloomy, but I could only feel the strength my father was giving me. I was closer than I'd ever been to him and it seemed unnatural to mourn – after all, if you are Christian, then you must believe that the dead depart for a better world. Home was depressing – full of long strained silences and lots of flowers – and I was almost relieved to go back to school. This was a very difficult period for my family, but I gained a strength from it that I have never really lost and an awareness that, since life can so unexpectedly be snatched from you, you have to make the best of it while it's there.

Worst days – giving you a belief in silver linings

It was undoubtedly as a result of my father's death that I resolved to pursue my swimming with a vengeance. I had already dedicated myself to working hard in the swimming pool, but the year that followed his loss saw my times for breaststroke tumble. I turned in best time after best time and qualified for the National Short Course Competition. Someone called Barry O'Brien won it, but I made the final and broke the one minute ten second barrier. That summer I qualified for the National Long Course Championships in Blackpool. But there was a large cloud on the horizon. One day my mother took me to one side. Being widowed so suddenly and at such a young age had been really hard on her and she had had a great deal to contend with. Having never had to balance a budget in her life, she was now forced to deal with accountants, solicitors, financial planning and complicated trust arrangements. It was clear that she was not quite sure how to put what she needed to say to me on that day. Eventually, after a bit of small talk, she came to the point: 'I can't afford to keep you at Millfield any longer.

What do you want to do?'

I knew exactly what I wanted to do. I wanted to swim. I realised how much time I had wasted and what a great opportunity Millfield had been for me. The school had the only full-time professional swimming coach in the country, and I quickly worked out that it was impossible to swim and continue further education in Britain. I was depressed. It seemed incomprehensible that there were so few coaches with enough water time to do the training necessary for British swimmers to make it to the top. I began to think that the only sensible long-term course was to give up swimming. Paddy Garrett, Millfield's swimming coach, knew, as usual, what was going on. He waited until he knew I was poised to throw in the towel and then offered me a little glimmer of hope. I was desperate and would have grasped at any straw given to me, however implausible it seemed. He knew it, and his timing was impeccable. 'Why don't you go to an American university?' he asked. Thanks to my outstanding academic prowess(!), I had never entertained the slightest thought of going to university and, even in the hopeless situation I found myself in, the very idea seemed ludicrous. But Paddy had it all worked out. He had arranged a meeting with Mr Jordan, an American teacher who had considerable knowledge of the US education system and who taught economics, which was the only subject I seemed to excel in.

Mr Jordan was passionate about his country and its universities, and I found myself being drawn in by what he was saying and his belief that I could get a place. After all, he knew my academic shortcomings so why would he waste his time if he didn't think there was at least a chance that I could get to one of the universities? He supplied some example exam papers and I realised I could do them. I began to get the feeling that perhaps, just perhaps, this was not quite the ludicrous idea I had first thought. I knew that David Wilkie (who was expected to – and subsequently did – win a gold medal in the 200-metre breaststroke at the Montreal Olympics) had gained a full athletic scholarship to the University of Miami. Apparently they paid for everything, which seemed like a good deal. There was one thing that confused me slightly, and that was why would Americans want to pick up all my education and living expenses for four years?

Whatever their reasons, I decided to see if I could qualify and make the most of their generosity, and I was soon booked in to take the SAT exam at the American Embassy in London. Paddy had dug out April's copy of the American publication *Swimming World*, which listed the results of the National Collegiate Athletic Association (NCAA) Swimming Championship and had an article on the top 12 swimming universities. We wrote to all of them and, to my delight, received fairly positive responses from the lot. The most enthusiastic was North Carolina State University, where the swimming coach, Don Easterling, offered me a full scholarship. I jumped at it. I knew that this was my only chance of getting to the Olympics.

During my four years at NC State Univerity, I began to appreciate the Americans' uncomplicated passion for excellence and how they could teach me to achieve it. This story sums it all up: at the beginning of October 1980, I visited North Carolina for a holiday, and Don asked me to be his guest at the North Carolina State University home-coming football game. 'We're going to put something right,' Don told me, and requested that I wear my Olympic blazer and bring my gold medal. There were 58,000 spectators in the crowd as the announcer's voice came over the loudspeaker system: 'When Duncan Goodhew was presented with his Olympic gold medal at Moscow, the British Union Jack wasn't raised and nor was his national anthem played. Today we intend to put that right.' With that, the 110-strong North Carolina State marching band began to play 'God Save the Queen'. The crowd got to their feet, and above the club house the Union Jack made its way up the flag pole. I stood there, stunned by this extraordinary display of sportsmanship. Here they were, a country who had missed out on the Olympic Games, honouring me, a foreigner, in such a grand and spirited way. Once the anthem finished, Don presented me with the medal. The crowd let out another cheer. I looked up at the thousands of faces and realised how lucky I had been to experience the extraordinary benefits of the American generosity of spirit. Had my family's circumstances not changed as dramatically as they did, it's very unlikely I would ever have ended up in an American university and learned from their whole approach to success and – most importantly – winning. The experience certainly taught me that, **if you seize the moment, difficulties can be turned into springboards of opportunity**.

Making the most of worst days

The backdrop to the 1980 Moscow Olympics was fairly unusual. The Russians had invaded Afghanistan in December 1979, and, in response, the US decided to boycott the Olympic Games. With the recently elected Margaret Thatcher behind the boycott, the British were divided into those who thought we should go and those who thought we shouldn't. Commentators and pundits alike were vocal, and we, the athletes, were in an impossible position. My stepfather, something of an establishment figure, believed that we should obey our government and join the boycott in support of Afghanistan. On the other hand, I, like all the other athletes, had worked for years to prepare for this event. What finally made me decide was the fact that at that time the only subjects about which there was a free flow of information were weather and sport. The world has changed beyond recognition since then with the internet revolution having taken place, but it seemed to me then that it was vital to carry on talking and to keep the channels of communication open. Having witnessed the workings of the common language of sport, there is no doubt in my mind that the Olympics had a far-reaching effect on Moscow and the rest of Russia, and I fervently believe that the Games had a great deal to do with letting the Soviet genie out of the bottle and hastening the arrival of *glasnost*.

If the politics leading up to the Games weren't traumatic enough, I also had a physical problem. It began with a dull ache at the very top of my shoulder nine weeks before the Olympics, and grew each day. I knew what was causing it. I had dived into too many shallow, poorly designed pools in Britain and pulled a tendon. The worsening pain was tendonitis, in which a calcium deposit crystallizes between the sheaths of tendon, and with every movement you make the flesh around the calcium crystal becomes more inflamed. The only cure is to rest. I had just those few weeks of training before the Olympics and did not know whether I could swim four hours a day with every stroke feeling as though a red hot needle was being pushed into my shoulder. However, I refused to let this put a stop to my training. Each session I kicked harder and faster, trying desperately to compensate for the lack of training my upper body was receiving. One afternoon, I kicked 20 sets of 200 metres and my legs were exhausted, but I pushed on. During that series I broke five pain barriers. As I kicked, the pain would rise from my shins, up my legs and then suddenly disappear as I drove on, ignoring it.

Once I had broken the pain barrier, my times became faster, confirming what I had realised for the past two years, that most of the time when I felt a bit jaded it was psychological. I had for some time made it a rule that however bad I felt, I always got up in the morning and went to the pool. The worse I felt the harder I worked. 99.9 per cent of the time, half-way through the work-out I would break through my fatigue, and my mood would improve along with my peformance. This technique carried my training beyond where I'd been before into new and uncharted territory. On a good day I would work on my technique, explore and fine tune what worked, and most of all enjoy the water and the challenge of the workout. There was never a moment to get bored. I felt the water, counted the strokes, watched the clock, relaxed the muscles

I didn't need to use and, of course, fought the pain. Working through the 'worst days' and forcing myself to keep going took me to new levels of achievement. It's the same for all of us. **You need to push your own limits in order to find out how much you can achieve**.

It is always worth looking within to see whether any of the restraints on your performance are self-induced and question whether the boundaries just in front of you are not worth pushing against. Perhaps you can achieve more than you have allowed yourself. If you have pushed yourself when it felt as though you were wrestling *against* the tide, think how much more you might achieve if you put in that kind of effort when you are swimming *with* the tide.

Worst days – harness your stress

We explored the problems associated with stress in Chapter 2, looking at its potentially destructive effect on your performance and your life. Being in an over-stressed state – quite apart from making you hell to live with – could be the death of you. But that's at one end of the scale.

At the other end of the scale, a moderate amount of stress can be helpful, with all those automatic fight or flight responses actually making a positive contribution to your performance. Some of the triggered stress responses are designed to make us perform: the right level of stress can provide us with the mental clarity or physical strength to achieve tasks which in normal unstressed situations we wouldn't even dream of. Think of people who produce their very best work under exam conditions or who are brilliant at public speaking although quite shy in small groups. I even heard of a woman who managed to shift a car single-handedly in order to free her son trapped underneath. She literally found superhuman energy through all the mechanisms triggered by the stress of her situation.

If you learn to listen to your body's responses to a stressful situation you put yourself in a position to harness a level of adrenalin

useful to your performance. So if, on a worst day, you feel particularly stressed and are paralysed by it, step back. Could your level of anxiety be controlled, put to good use and turned into something constructive?

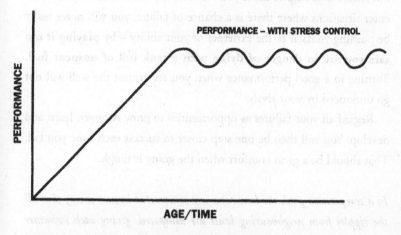

When worst days turn into worst weeks

Worst days shouldn't go on for ever. If you have so many bad days in a row that you can't remember what a good one even feels like, there is a danger that you may actually be suffering from depression and require professional help. Unlike women, who tend to talk about their worries and emotions openly and easily, men often put on a brave face and conceal what they are feeling. For this reason, men can be depressed and yet be unaware of it, and can easily attribute symptoms like lethargy and anger to factors such as overwork. In reality, the causes could be more sinister. To a man it can seem a loss of face, a failing or a weakness to acknowledge that anything at all is wrong. But however strong the defence system you have built up, clinical depression calls for outside help, and you shouldn't be afraid or embarrassed to seek it. A self-help book will not be enough to dig you out of the deepest doldrums.

Comfort for your 'off' days

Max Beerbohm said: 'There is much to be said for failure. It is more interesting than success.' You may not always feel like agreeing with this, but failure does help to move you forward. If you never attempt tasks or enter situations where there is a chance of failure, you will never really be pushing yourself to the extremes of your ability – **by playing it too safe you are in danger of dying with a tank full of unspent fuel**. Turning in a good performance when you are against the wall will not go unnoticed by your rivals.

Regard all your failures as opportunities to grow stronger, learn and develop. You will then be one step closer to success each time you fail. That should be a great comfort when the going is tough.

In a competition pool, the lane ropes are constructed in such a way that all the ripples from neighbouring lanes are dissipated, giving each swimmer calm, undisturbed water to swim in – these are known as 'wave-breakers'. It's always worth checking whether your wave-breakers are securely fastened. Are they efficient at isolating waves and turbulence in one lane and keeping them out of the others? Or are they not really doing their job? If the latter is the case, any problems you are having in one area might be destroying your performance in others. Efficient wave-breakers will ensure that you are able to focus on what matters.

Action

- Review your responses to Chapter 4's action points.
- Look at your swimming lanes and chart which way the water is flowing in each – against you or with you.
- Write down what you have learned when things seemed to be going against you.
- Write down how you can apply the experiences you've learned in one lane to your goals in another.

● Write down the 'partitions' or actions that you employ as wave-breakers between your lanes.

CHAPTER 6

MAKING A SPLASH

Step Six:
Build and Defend
Your Self-Confidence

Confidence is the most elusive of qualities – one day you're overflowing with the stuff, the next it's just a dim memory. If you play golf you'll know exactly what I mean. **Yesterday you were Tiger Woods, today you're in the rough battling to keep your ball on the fairway**. But why? Confidence has a lot to do with it, and nurturing that fragile creature in any way you can – through tried and tested methods as well as in ways that are particularly suited to you – is essential if you want to feel buoyant and get the most out of life.

The idea that you need to have a Positive Mental Attitude (PMA) in order to win is one of the oldest messages in the self-help canon. PMA will not just help your mental state, it will have a beneficial effect on your physical condition too. This in turn will sustain your self-confidence and ability to perform . . . and so the cycle continues. If your mental attitude is negative, however, you are likely to release stress hormones that have entirely the opposite effect.

Losing It

Loss of confidence is sometimes the single reason that we lose – if we don't believe winning is a possibility then we unconsciously put failure on the agenda. Losing your bottle, your self-belief, the courage of your convictions – call it what you will but it amounts to the same thing and always gives the same outcome: a greater chance of failure and loss of motivation.

Sometimes we lose faith in ourselves because a number of different factors are not quite as we want them and we get put off our stride and distracted. If we don't have some defence mechanisms in place to stop certain situations or people getting to us, the whole fabric can unravel. One of the first experiences I had of this was in my early days of competing at national level when a whole sequence of circumstances combined to sweep even a corner of the winning carpet from under my feet. It was during my last term at public school that I had my first encounter with David Wilkie, who was to become my number one swimming rival in the years that followed, and who from the first day I encountered him always succeeded in undermining my faith in myself. It got to the point where the very sight of him could send me into a state of near paralysis in which I could do anything but justice to my swimming potential.

As well as being psychologically outgunned by Wilkie on that first encounter, I had problems with the kind of pool we were swimming in. It was a day when mental challenge met physical challenge and my confidence literally drowned in the tidal wave. It was the kind of day we can all have when someone close to us observes our behaviour, makes the diagnosis and rather acutely (if annoyingly) observes: 'Nothing's right today is it?' Of course, there might be nothing tangibly wrong at all, it's just a general feeling of malaise and a lack of belief in yourself. The day in question was during The British National Swimming Championships. The full contingent of swimming greats were there, including Wilkie, Paul Naisby (both back from training in the United States) and David Leigh. The championships were being held in Blackpool in a salt-water pool in which eight lanes had been squashed into six (so the black lines were not in the centre of the lanes). The other swimmers apparently loved it, but to me it was like swimming in split pea soup and the saline content, as well as making my eyes bloodshot, made me too buoyant, lifting my legs higher in the water than I was used to and making my feet break the surface. Incredibly, to cap it all there was no electronic timekeeping system, which meant that the timing had to be judged visually by three timekeepers at the end of each of the lanes, leaving the final decision on placing to the referee. This was definitely not what I had expected at a national championship.

I got through to the finals of the 100-metre breaststroke and found myself sitting there waiting for the final with Naisby, Leigh and Wilkie. It was not a comfortable experience. Wilkie laughed and joked and seemed to know the result of the race before it had even been swum. Any confidence I had evaporated in the face of his, leaving me with a sense of desperation at my impending defeat. The desperation remained with me throughout the race. I clawed at the water trying to force my body to do what my mind dreamt of but knew I could not achieve. I lost that relaxed stroke I had achieved at the Coca-Cola International earlier in the year and, because of the force I was using, tightness soon set into my muscles and my stroke shortened. This was followed by exhaustion, and then pain. Touching the end was a relief from the physical discomfort but not from the knowledge of complete defeat. I had been beaten before I was even wet, but it was going to take me some time to learn that lesson. I had allowed the environment to overpower me, the other competitors to get under my skin and . . . well, need I continue? Quite simply, I made every excuse in the book to myself for failing, but the real reason for it all was that I had been stripped bare of my confidence. What I needed to grasp was the lesson that Eleanor Roosevelt put so well: **'No one can make you feel inferior without your consent.'** She's absolutely right, I just hadn't learnt it yet.

Personal confidence trips

What I required, as we all do on certain occasions, was to find a way to change my mental approach. I had to discover some kind of mechanism that would allow me to lock away all the doubts I had about winning and put me in exactly the right frame of mind for competition. Different methods work for each us – I remember a particularly flamboyant approach among the Canadians at the Commonwealth Games. The whole team were raucous – most of all a swimmer called Graham Smith, who prowled around kicking chairs and looking menacing before races began. Everyone, including myself, gave him a wide berth, but I did try his aggressive approach (omitting the chair-kicking, I hasten to add). What I discovered, of course, was that his approach couldn't be mine. Outward aggression simply wasn't my style, so I decided to try an inwardly aggressive attitude – as I had by now grasped the fact that winning is as much about your psychological state as your physical skills.

I will come on to some techniques later in this chapter; suffice it to say that **there are ways of bolstering confidence that may be as individual to you as your DNA.** We need to discover what or who our confidence props are. One of the key players in buoying up my own confidence at the time of the Moscow Olympics was Wilbur Smith. I've never met the man – I wouldn't know him from Adam – but he certainly helped me win a gold medal. In the weeks leading up to the 1980 Olympics I was aware that if I experienced the same stress levels as in Montreal four years earlier, I wouldn't stand a chance of winning in a heat, let alone the whole race. I knew I had to keep myself under control. Journeys to the aquatic centre in Moscow involved a 40-minute drive across the city and we had learned to sit at the front of the Russian bus, as it had a less than effective exhaust system that leaked noxious gases into the interior. The fumes weren't going to improve anyone's performance! What I needed during these journeys was a cocoon, a mental hideaway where I could go to isolate myself from the mounting stress. Enter Wilbur Smith to help me rise above the Olympic pressure. As my coach always said: 'The hay's in the barn.' Now it was time to wait patiently and conserve every physical movement in an attempt to keep up my energy reserves. I also needed to stay calm and conserve my emotional energy, to prevent nervous tightening of the muscles and maintain absolute control. **We all have to play the waiting game from time to time and it's then that the stress can mount and self-doubt get on top of us**. For me it was vital that nothing should erode the confidence that in a few hours' time would carry me to the top step of the rostrum and the long sought-after dream of an Olympic gold medal. Reading a thriller enabled me to maintain my equilibrium and sustain my confidence. It meant that I could keep my head down, avoid conversation and be utterly absorbed in a world apart from my own situation. If I'd been distracted by so much as a short conversation, the slightest that was said could have exposed me to the risk of a massive loss of confidence.

How to make confidence hang around

One of the best ways to boost your confidence is by achieving your goals. What better way to give yourself a lift than being able to tick off something on your list of targets or to see that you have come a distance.

In order to do this you must constantly review your goals and remind yourself of what you are planning to achieve. But beware! It's all too easy to dip your toe in and then pull back – the unfamiliarity can deter you. New experiences can feel odd – just like the imperfect golf swing you tried to change. Look at it the other way round – new projects: and actions *need* to feel odd – if they aren't new.

Action, I firmly believe, is the antidote to despair, so if you are experiencing a lack of confidence, the one sure way to boost it is to take some practical and positive steps towards making the changes in your life that I have outlined in this book. If, for example, you take a healthier approach to your own fitness, and review your life to ensure that it has balance in all areas, you should find that your self-assurance grows – both out of a sense of achievement and out of a sense of direction. And once this becomes incorporated into the routine of your life, your confidence should continue to grow by the day.

Be happy to stand out

'When you're as great as I am, it's hard to be humble.'

These words could *only* have come from Muhammed Ali. We all got used to his special brand of arrogance, and it was hard not to be amused by it. It was harder still not to believe in his supremacy. He knew he was the best, and for years no one could really challenge him. His confidence never waned, and he lived and breathed his simple claim: 'I am the greatest.' He knew that winning wasn't about being one of the crowd – and he wasn't afraid of his position, or of defending his right to be at the top. Self-doubt was not in his dictionary. Self-confidence was. What must it have been like to face him in the ring? For a long period, his opponents didn't have a chance. He advertised his unassailability to such an extent that before the opposition even began to fight against him, they had lost.

Putting yourself in the lead involves an understanding that you have to be out on a limb to be the best. Winning is not about being one of the crowd. It's not about asking 'why me?' when you are out in front or querying your right to be there. At the Amateur Athletic Union National Swimming Championships in Los Angeles in 1976, I found myself doing just that – doubting my right to be in a winning position, and in some extraordinary way it was this self-doubt that held me back. The gun had gone off, sending us into action for the 100 metres final. Initially it felt good. I seemed to slip effortlessly through the water and there was nothing in my mind but the task in hand. As I came to the surface to breathe on each stroke, I was vaguely aware of the crowd and the commentary coming over the PA system. There were only 15 metres left to swim, and as my head broke the surface of the water I heard just two words: 'Duncan Goodhew'. I knew instantly that I was ahead, and the reality of the situation sent my mind into turmoil. I was ahead of Wilkie and Henken, the two world-record holders. Me, no one from nowhere. I asked myself the question that seemed to burn into my very soul: 'Why me?' As I did, I knew I was losing it. My stroke tightened with the physical effort I was making to try and combat this negative thought process. Why should I be the best in the world? Think of the probability against it. Despite my stroke falling apart, I hung in there desperately trying to force my way through the water. I touched the end wall and looked at the time clock. I had come in third, behind Wilkie and Henken. It was a time that would have won in the previous Olympic Games, and I had even cut 3.8 seconds off my best from the previous year. It also meant that my dream had come true and I would be going to the Olympic Games. But I hadn't come first – I hadn't reached out and grabbed it.

If I'd been born and brought up in America, where they believe that talent can happen to anyone, I wouldn't have questioned my right to win even for a split second. The American way is to strive for excellence and never question the right to attain it. At NC State I learnt how highly the social status of winning is valued in the US. At the end of the nineteenth century, American universities adopted the philosophy of 'healthy body, healthy mind'. They also recognised the great camaraderie and sense of belonging that sport develops in spectators and players alike and, more commercially, they realised that success in sport could be effective self-promotion for the university.

All this taught me that **you should never feel embarrassed about being competitive, never feel guilty about winning and that the laurels are there for the picking**. Doing your best, even if it means being better than other people, should always be your highest aim. If you've given your all in the spirit of competition, you have lost to no man. This is a maxim held by many a sportsman and always reminds me that even if you don't come first, you'll have improved, taken yourself to your own furthest limits and grown in confidence. If you lose you learn. And then there is the next time when your 'all' could get you there.

Self-talk and self publicity

Even if you don't shout about it as loudly as Muhammed Ali, you need to tell yourself and others that you are 'the best'. The British taste for reticence, however, makes many of us feel uncomfortable about bragging to the world about our talents. As a nation we tend to make something of a fine art out of hiding our light under a bushel. Perhaps when it's described in the following way, the whole notion of self-publicity becomes more palatable: **'Modesty is the art of encouraging people to find out for themselves how wonderful you are.'** Strategic self-promotion can be very effective. In the sporting arena you can pick your venues and fixtures in order to get yourself noticed by the right audience and the right competitors. In a corporate context you might need to raise awareness of your value if you think it is being underestimated. One of the most effective ways of going about this is by involving a head-hunter – a job offer from another company is a good way of getting your company to recognise your talents, and in any job or pay review you will then be negotiating from a position of strength.

In sport and business it is essential that the opposition believes you are the best – but you also have to believe it yourself. The English are particularly good at self-deprecation, but in certain situations it is extremely unhelpful – and, indeed, can make you a walkover. Not only does putting yourself down become a habit which is hard to break but it is also a guaranteed route to failure. **If you tell others you're useless they will believe it, you'll start to believe it yourself and it will become true**. People then expect only uselessness of you, and you will play up to the role. It's the perfect self-fulfilling prophecy.

If you've got into this habit, the first thing that has to go is negative talk. Are you the kind of person who describes a glass as 'half empty' or are you the more positive 'half full' type? Attitude and the language that goes with it can play an important role in determining the outcome of your plans and projects. If you constantly undermine yourself by saying: 'I won't get that contract' or 'I can't possibly get that job', are you giving yourself the best chance? If you use positive language and say to yourself, 'I *will* win that contract' or, 'I'm *going* to get that job', both you and those around you will have higher expectations, and the likelihood that you will succeed is hugely increased. It sounds so simple, but it works. Try it.

Whether or not you choose to say any of these things out loud, the process of reminding yourself of what you can achieve is remarkably effective. **Constantly telling yourself that you can achieve almost anything at all if you are determined enough can take you half way towards the finishing line**.

My most successful use of self-talk ever was when I talked myself into winning the 100-metre breaststroke final at the Moscow Olympics. I sensed the stress level around me rising, but I was calm and relaxed, and I hoped my rivals would see this calmness and interpret it as confidence. When it was time, we marched out onto the pool side, and once behind the block I started to work myself up into the competitive frenzy that I had rehearsed so often. Every motion was familiar, and the only hint that it was the real thing this time was when I thrust my hands into my robe pockets with such force that one of them ripped. The whistle went. Everything was now on automatic pilot. I eased into the first few strokes and at the 25-metre mark felt myself slipping back in the field. To make up the ground I'd lost, I powered into the turn and exploded off the wall. I knew it had been a great turn, and I then hit my stroke with everything I had – but suddenly it seemed that my stroke spun out of control like the tyres of a car accelerating too fast. With 25 metres to go, I heard myself saying: 'Duncan if you don't do something right now you are not going to win, and that is totally absurd.'

My total being focused on the end of the pool. I was only metres away from the touch pad at the end. Everything then clicked. My legs sent my body surging forwards and I flung myself towards the pad as if I was going to swim through it. I grabbed the backstroke handles that stuck out from the side of the block, and when I turned round, confirmed what I already knew in my heart, that I had indeed won an Olympic gold. They say that when you drown your whole life passes in front of your eyes. In this case I was probably drowning in my own emotions, and images of all the arduous training, my family, my coaches and my team-mates flooded in front of me. I had a feeling of total fulfilment that made me glow inside. If I hadn't spoken those sharp words to myself I certainly wouldn't have made it, and my decade of dreaming would have gone unfulfilled.

Visualisation and emotionalisation

Self-talk works hand in hand with visualisation and emotionalisation, techniques much used in competitive sport and also invaluable tools in ordinary life. First of all, work on your action replays. Imagine reliving your greatest achievements – those that best display your qualities and talents. Then, **before you attempt to reach your goal, imagine that you have already achieved it**. Think what it will be like to win. By doing this you will already have rehearsed the situation and subconsciously you will be demonstrating your right to win. In a business environment, it is often important to play things fairly cool, so that, for example, you treat the winning of a contract or the closing of a deal as a natural right, rather than something you are surprised at. Appearing to be calm and collected in the winning situation is vital if you are not to undermine the confidence of your client. If you are clearly flabbergasted at your good fortune, your client or customer will start to feel doubtful about your experience and indeed your right to be in the winning position.

I used this approach time and time again to good effect when I was swimming. I would mentally rehearse a race until physically going through with it would sometimes feel like just a formality. At the beginning of 1980, I made time out of the water to dream about the perfect race. The perfect start. The number of strokes to the first length. The perfect turn. The number of strokes to the second length. Every swim I did, I analysed my approach, not only physically but also psychologically. By the time I reached the final of the breaststroke race in July, everything was in place. I had imagined myself into first place and the only thing required was actually to execute it. Sounds simple? I already felt I was half-way there.

Love your enemies – but give them a wide berth

We've talked about how to sustain your self-confidence by believing in yourself; another important element is getting others to believe in you. You may have worked on the basis that your family and friends will be the people who always support you through thick and thin. If you are lucky this will be the case. But for some of you, the people closest to you may actually be the most negative influence in your life. Your nearest and dearest probably have the most to lose if your situation changes in any way and if you want to make any adjustments to your life the niggling voices that say: 'Don't do it', 'You can't do it', 'Why bother?' could well be theirs. When people warn you against changing the status quo, or tell you that you are taking a big risk, question their motivation. Ironically, it is often those closest to you who find it hardest to swallow not just change in your life, but more specifically your successes. Gore Vidal sums this up perfectly: 'Whenever a friend succeeds, a little something in me dies,' he says. How staggeringly honest of him – and haven't we all occasionally observed the slightest of shivers when we tell a friend or relative of an achievement?

A key factor in your confidence-building mission is to eliminate doubt, and this might involve excluding the doubting Thomases in your life – or at least learning to ignore them. Rosemary Conley's advice on the matter is fairly straightforward: 'If you have negative friends, get rid of them, if you have negative staff, fire them, but if you have negative family – then you have a problem . . .'

As well as negative family and friends, with whom you need to deal sensitively, there are your more obvious 'enemies'. There's often someone in your life, either an overt rival or simply someone in your office or your social life, with whom you don't see eye to eye. My *bête noire* during my swimming career, as I've mentioned, was David Wilkie, the top dog who saw me as the young pretender who needed to be kept in his place. To the shock of commentators and audiences alike, I beat him in a regional swimming meet in the US. The next time I saw him after that, my greeting was returned with the words: 'F*** off, you little p****.'

Wilkie waged subtle (and sometimes not so subtle) but effective, psychological warfare on me for several years. Even during the Olympics, although we were in the same team, the rivalry was intense, and he seemed to go out of his way to undermine me at every opportunity. On one occasion when I went to find him for a practice session, he was lying on his bed reading a book and looking excessively calm and relaxed. He was so under control it was unnerving, and by taking his time to get ready to go down to the pool he managed to agitate me further. Here we were, both wanting to win for Great Britain, yet only one of us could achieve the ultimate – an Olympic gold medal. At the meal just before we left for the final of the 100-metre breaststroke, he sat down opposite me. As I was about to start eating he looked at what I had on my tray and said: 'You'll sink.' 'I don't like getting nervous on an empty stomach,' I replied. Why did he have to sit near me? I would have enjoyed a solitary meal to retain my composure before the big moment. When I eventually looked up, Wilkie was still sitting there, and he persisted in sticking by me right until the race (in which he broke away at the last minute, touching the end of the pool before I did).

I never really got my feelings about him under control, but I did eventually put them into perspective. It might take time to become immune to the efforts of certain individuals in your life to undermine you, but what matters is that they don't strip you of your confidence. **Take a step back and look objectively at what they might be trying to do. In a competitive business environment there will be people who set out to expose your weaknesses or undermine your confidence: be aware of their intentions, have intimate knowledge of their weaknesses and always watch for the sprint finish**. Have faith that your innate abilities, credibility that you have methodically built up and carefully planned hard work will stand you in good stead.

Who champions the champions?

So we've made ourselves immune to the effects of our negative friends and enemies. Now let's turn to the champions. As far as possible, you should surround yourself with positive people whose objectives are mutual support and success. Your own feelings of self-worth can be hugely influenced by the kind of people you mix with. It helps enormously during periods of self-doubt if there is someone who continues to believe in you even when you don't believe in yourself. If you have someone encouraging you to reach your goals isn't it more likely that you'll reach them? These are the people with whom you celebrate the small and big things and who are with you as you move on to the next stage in your life. While considering who plays this role in your life, it's worth asking whether you play it in someone else's – as well as being hugely valuable to the other person, it teaches you more about yourself.

I have had a number of champions during my life, but one of the most significant was Don Easterling, the charismatic swimming team coach at NC State. He was clever at exploiting our strengths and weaknesses in order to help us reach our goals; we needed a relationship like this in order to get results, and Don's trust and belief in us commanded our respect. Soon after I arrived on the campus I went up to meet him, and our first encounter set the tone of the relationship. As I entered the lobby space I saw a large group of swimmers standing listening intently to a man with sandy blonde hair. He was good-looking, with sharp features and fiery eyes, and judging by the way the swimmers were listening to him, he was a showman who loved an audience. We made small talk, but I was impatient. I could feel the time ticking by – the Montreal Olympics were less than a year away and I needed to get into the water. 'I think I need some help with my stroke,' I said. 'When do we get into the water?' 'Not until the last week of September,' he replied. Another three weeks lost. Since Millfield I had suffered from a recurring knee injury and it was the fear of triggering this that stopped me making the changes to my stroke that, deep down inside, I knew I had to make if I was to fulfil my ambitions. It wasn't so much fear of the injury itself but of what it would do to my swimming career. If it flared up badly, it would be the end of the Olympic dream and would prevent me from continuing the one thing in my life that seemed to make sense and had kept me together. It was for these reasons that I was so impatient to get going.

Coach made it a rule to allow all his swimmers to settle in at school before he started the work-outs – they generally needed to let off steam and get acclimatised to being back in the classroom after the long summer break. Don had met Millfield coach Paddy Garrett in London while coaching the US team for the Coca-Cola Internationals. The American had been impressed by the English coach, but what Paddy had said about the English boy now sitting in front of him in North Carolina was hard to swallow. For a start, his times were extremely marginal and Don had had a hard time justifying the cost of giving him a scholarship . . . but he could sense there was something different about this bald-headed Englishman who sat there looking anaemically white, intense and impatient. Perhaps he could help this odd-looking boy fulfil his potential. Easterling lived for that. A young, talented athlete coming to him and asking for a chance to be the best. He knew they needed someone to believe in them and to encourage them to take the steps needed to succeed.

The first time I swam in front of him was clearly critical. He watched me with amazement as I swam freestyle up and down the pool, thinking to himself: 'This boy's stroke is short and ungainly, and he has no technique; even his tumble turns are a mess.' He noticed the raw power I used to get through the water and walked up and down the side of the pool, glancing at two other swimmers who were gliding effortlessly through the water, only further emphasising my lack of technique. It seemed an eternity before we changed to breaststroke.

In his whole career, he had never seen a competitive swimmer who swam breaststroke like me. It looked even worse than my freestyle – if that's possible. Perhaps he had been conned. Coach asked me to do another 50 yards, and I noticed him timing it. When I finished, he asked me to do another 50 and then another. This continued for some while, and each time I came in and touched the wall, I noticed that the blank look on his face was slowly changing to one of incredulity. Eventually he asked me to get out and sat me down on the pool-side bench. He looked at me in bewilderment, slowly shaking his head from side to side. He looked troubled. 'God dammit,' he said 'you really *do* swim like that . . .' He seemed to be wrestling with the reality of what he had just said 'If, and I mean *if*, you can swim the times you say you can swim with a stroke like that, then we're going places,' he continued.

I felt a prickle of excitement rising in me. This man was bitten. I could feel it. And he'd seen what I knew was there in me. We worked on changing my stroke over the next two weeks. Don Easterling became the best champion I could ever have hoped for – he was strict when I needed to be pushed and reassuring when I needed to be nurtured.

Crowd support

Support doesn't always come in the form of an individual, however. It might be that a group of people can galvanise you to successful action. I witnessed this once in a very raw form when I watched a young swimmer called Steve Holland beat the world 1500-metre record back in 1975. The support he got from the crowd had an extraordinary power all of its own which drove him on. The 1500 metres doesn't usually cause a stir, but there had been a rumour that Steve Holland was going for a new world record and it must have spread beyond the swimmers to the audience filling the stands. The young, slightly-built Australian boy seemed to bounce off the walls at each end of the pool. Up and down the pool he went, while many of his fellow swimmers religiously took down his time at each end.

He had started off well but then appeared not to be able to keep the pace up. Disappointment began to grip the audience. We had all wanted to see the world record broken, to witness the human race excelling itself. Steve still had 30 lengths to swim and never let the pace slip enough for us to lose hope. It was at the half-way point that he started to increase his speed. Each length was faster than the one before, and soon he had made up the lost ground and was back on schedule to break the world record. The ripples of excitement grew, carrying from the swimmers to the spectators. Competitors started to move to the poolside. I was drawn magnetically towards the pool to get a good look at this teenager wrestling with himself. He had left his opposition way behind and it was now a battle of self-will over fatigue. By the last length almost everyone was on their feet. The world record was within his reach and we were all willing him on. As he touched the end there was a momentary pause in the cheering as all eyes flicked to the automatic scoreboard and when, a few seconds later, the time flickered up onto the screen the crowd went crazy. It was a new world record.

The crowd had literally spurred him on to victory. It was electrifying to witness. Because they believed so strongly that he could do it, Steve Holland took on the power of their belief and swam the race of his life. You too can tap into the energy of your 'team'. **With a network of mutually supportive colleagues, friends and family you can achieve a great deal more than if you perceive yourself as a lone ranger – one man against the world.** Your team, which may also comprise clients and customers, will give you feedback – ask them how you are doing for a free assessment of how you rate, and then act on it.

Push yourself

Many of us experience a degree of paranoia about being 'found out' or discovered not to be the person we have set ourself up to be. As we age, that concern might intensify, making us play safe and stay in our 'comfort zone', sticking to what we feel comfortable with – treading water in effect.

Youthfulness comes from a sense of adventure, not from sticking at the same comfortable point of achievement until you die. If you don't keep pushing forward when you're in your pool, you drop to the bottom. Is that really your ambition?

You can, however, experience a huge boost to your self-confidence if you push out your own boundaries – and remind yourself what you are capable of. Think of it as a huge mental and physical stretch – your big stretch. It could be any of the following: taking a calculated risk, making yourself confront a fear (and realising that you can survive it) or learning something new. All these are confidence-building tricks that give you a tremendous sense of power, achievement and personal development. When you have mastered something that you had a hang-up about, not only do you feel great, but you also look for the next challenge, so you're still growing as an individual. There's no need to stop learning just because you're out of college. There's no moment in your life when you should stop developing and pushing yourself. If the only time you stretch your legs is when you sit down with your cosily slippered feet in front of the fire, then you are on a fast-track to an unsatisfying, complacent and premature old age.

By using the big stretch you become more powerful and self-confident and by constantly reminding yourself what you are capable of you will extend your boundaries. The more you test yourself, the more powerful and self-assured you will become.

Anyone taking part in competition sport recognises that being physically honed by training is not enough. Encouragement from a coach and enthusiasm from supporters will be the added elements that help them go the distance. If all things are in place, dive in – and to hell with the competition! You can win if you want to.

Action

- Review your responses to Chapter 5's action points.
- Where would you place your current confidence on a scale of 1-10? What would be a comfortable level of confidence for you? What would you need to do to move it up one notch? Record your answers and review periodically.
- Next to your swimming lanes write down who and what erodes your confidence and causes the current to flow against you.
- Conduct the same exercise for who or what builds your confidence and makes the current flow with you.
- Identify your team for each of the swimming lanes – and make a note of your adversaries.
- Look outside your normal frame of reference for coaches, mentors and useful organisations, and add them to your swimming lanes.
- Write down some 'big stretches' that will take you out of your comfort zone.
- Think of your past and current successes and ask yourself how you promote them.
- Revisit your plans for celebration – and add in with whom you'll be celebrating.

CONCLUSION

This book is all about **you**. We hope the messages have inspired you to take a better aim for your second half. You owe it to yourself not to tread water. Aspire to better things: new energy, new balance and the enjoyment of new challenges are all within your grasp. Go back over everything you have noted down in your pad. This is your contract, and you owe it to yourself to fulfil it.

- So you now aim to have a life that suits **you**
- So you find new motivation
- So you learn and develop
- So you feel energised
- So you stretch out to meet your goals

So now you won't sink – you'll swim

You've fixed your life!

If you would like further help, log on to: www.duncangoodhew.com

Appendix I

Extracts from: Coronary Heart Disease Statistics – British Heart Foundation Database 2000

- Heart and circulatory disease is the UK's biggest killer.
- Death rates from coronary heart disease in the UK are among the highest in the world.
- Over 1.5 million people in the UK have angina and half a million have heart failure, and these numbers are rising.

Cardiovascular disease (CVD) is the main cause of death in the UK, accounting for over 250,000 deaths a year – more than four out of ten of all deaths. The main forms of CVD are coronary heart disease (CHD) and stroke. About half of all deaths from CVD are from CHD and about a quarter are from stroke.

CVD is also the main cause of premature death: approximately 40 per cent of premature deaths in men and 30 per cent of premature deaths in women.

Nearly all deaths from CHD are because of a heart attack. Over 270,000 people in the UK suffer a heart attack each year. About half are fatal. In about 30 per cent of heart attacks the patient dies before reaching hospital.

CHD comes in two main forms: heart attack and angina. Angina is a pain in the chest brought on by exercise or emotion. It can be mild or severe and generally lasts less than ten minutes. A heart attack causes similar pain but lasts longer and can be fatal. Angina is caused by a narrowing of the blood vessels to the heart muscle. A heart attack results when one of those vessels is entirely blocked by a blood clot.

Smoking: An estimated 20 per cent of deaths from CHD in men and 17 per cent in women are due to smoking. Until recently the proportion of adult cigarette smokers had been decreasing rapidly but the decline has now levelled off. About 28 per cent of men and 26 per cent of women in the UK still smoke.

Diet: One reason why CHD rates are high in the UK is because the average diet is so unhealthy. In particular, fat intake – especially of saturated fat – in the UK is too high, and fruit and vegetable consumption is too low.

Physical activity: Physical activity lowers the risk of CHD. The activity needs to be regular, of moderate intensity and rhythmic, such as brisk walking, dancing or cycling. It is estimate that in the UK about 36 per cent of deaths from CHD in men and 38 per cent of deaths from CHD in women are related to lack of physical activity. It is recommended that adults should aim for at least 30 minutes of moderate activity on five or more days of the week. Only 37 per cent of men and 25 per cent of women are active at this level.

Alcohol: Moderate alcohol consumption (one or two drinks a day) is associated with reduced risk of CHD. At high levels of intake – particularly in binges – the risk of CHD is increased. The Government recommends sensible drinking levels of no more than 21 units a week for men and 14 for women. Overall 38 per cent of men and 21 per cent of women in Great Britain consume more alcohol than the weekly recommended levels, but these figures are rising.

Psychosocial well-being: A number of psychosocial factors are associated with an increased risk of CHD. These include inadequate social support or lack of social networks, work stress (especially where work combines high demand with low control), depression (including anxiety) and personality (particularly hostility).

Overweight and obesity: Overweight is associated with raised blood pressure, raised blood cholesterol, non-insulin diabetes and low levels of physical activity. Overweight individuals therefore have an increased risk of CHD. About 46 per cent of men and 32 per cent of women are overweight in England, and a further 17 per cent of men and 21 per cent of women are obese.

Blood pressure: Risk of CHD is directly related to both systolic and diastolic blood pressure levels. Blood pressure levels are high in the UK. About 41 per cent of men and 33 per cent of women either have raised blood pressure or are being treated for raised blood pressure. The prevalence of high blood pressure increases with age in both men and women.

Blood cholesterol: Risk of CHD is directly related to blood cholesterol levels, and it is estimated that in the UK 45 per cent of deaths from CHD in men and 47 per cent of deaths from CHD in women are due to a raised blood cholesterol level.

Diabetes: Diabetes substantially increases the risk of CHD: people with diabetes have around three times as much risk of developing CHD as those without the disease.

Appendix II

Extracts from: Smoking and Your Heart – British Heart Foundation

How stopping smoking will help your heart: Carbon monoxide and nicotine are the two chemicals in tobacco smoke that probably have the most effect on your heart. Carbon monoxide joins onto the red protein of the blood cell called haemoglobin, reducing its ability to carry oxygen to the heart and all other parts of the body. In some smokers, up to half of the blood can be carrying carbon monoxide instead of oxygen, depriving the heart of vital oxygen. Nicotine stimulates the body to produce adrenalin, which makes the heart beat faster and raises the blood pressure, causing the heart to work harder. Other components of cigarette smoke appear to damage the lining of the coronary arteries and lead to atherosclerosis.

It is the tar in cigarettes that causes cancer. However, if a cigarette is low in tar it does not necessarily mean that the amount of nicotine and carbon monoxide is reduced. So low tar cigarettes can be just as harmful to your heart.

Cigarette smoking has dangerous effects on other parts of the body as well as the heart:

- Eighteen in every 100 stroke deaths are associated with smoking.
- Four out of every five lung cancer deaths are caused by smoking.
- Smoking is also associated with cancer of the larynx, bladder, kidneys, cervix, oesophagus, stomach and duodenum.

- Smoking can lead to chronic bronchitis and emphysema.
- Smoking can lead to diseases of the arteries in the legs
  (peripheral arterial disease), which can in turn lead to the need
  for amputation.

The rising risk: The risk of heart attack rises with the amount you smoke. In general, people who smoke cigarettes have about twice as great a risk of a heart attack as people who do not. However, this increased risk is particularly large in smokers aged under 50: their heart attack death rates are up to ten times greater than non-smokers of the same age. The more you smoke and the younger you started, the greater your risk.

Appendix III

Extracts from: Physical Activity and your Heart – British Heart Foundation

What causes coronary heart disease? Coronary heart disease is caused when the arteries supplying blood to the heart (the coronary arteries) become narrowed by a gradual build-up of fatty material within their walls. This condition is called 'atherosclerosis' and the fatty material is called 'atheroma'. The disease can suddenly become worse if a blood clot forms over the atheroma (a thrombosis). This is what causes a heart attack.

The atheroma develops when cholesterol is taken up by cells in the coronary artery walls where the narrowing process begins. This cholesterol is formed from the fats in the foods you eat. Two types of cholesterol are involved: LDL cholesterol, which forms the atheroma, and HDL cholesterol, which removes cholesterol from the circulation and appears to protect against coronary heart disease. The goal is to have an overall low level of total cholesterol, with a low level of LDL cholesterol and a higher level of the protective HDL cholesterol.

Risk factors for coronary heart disease: There are several known 'risk factors' for heart disease that you can do something about. (A 'risk factor' is something that increases people's risk of getting the disease.) The major risk factors are smoking, high blood pressure, high blood cholesterol and physical inactivity. Other lifestyle factors may also play a part, including drinking too much alcohol, excessive salt intake and obesity.

Physical inactivity is probably the most common risk factor for heart disease in the UK. Surveys have shown that seven out of ten adults in the UK do not take enough regular physical activity to achieve health benefits to protect their heart. And yet, even though physical inactivity is so common, eight out of every ten adults think they are fit.

Why is physical activity so important for your heart?: Exactly how and why physical activity plays such an important part in preventing coronary heart disease is still the subject of research. However, it appears to act in the following ways:

- Physical activity helps improve your blood cholesterol levels. It seems to raise HDL cholesterol (the 'protective' cholesterol) but does not affect LDL cholesterol levels. However, in order to maintain the benefit in HDL cholesterol, you have to make sure that you do regular physical activity.
- It helps prevent blood clotting. A heart attack usually occurs when blood clots form over atheroma in the coronary arteries. Regular exercise helps to prevent blood clotting.
- It helps to lower high blood pressure and prevent high blood pressure from developing. High blood pressure is one of the four major risk factors for coronary heart disease. In nine out of ten people with high blood pressure there is no single underlying cause. However, unhealthy lifestyle plays an important part. In particular being overweight or obese, eating too much salt, drinking too much alcohol and physical inactivity can all raise blood pressure. Regular, moderate rhythmic exercise, such as walking or swimming, helps to reduce blood pressure in people with high blood pressure. This sort of exercise may also prevent high blood pressure from developing.

Appendix IV

Extracts from: Eating for your Heart – British Heart Foundation

How what you eat and drink affects you heart: Following a healthy diet can substantially reduce the risk of developing heart disease, and can also increase the chances of survival after a heart attack. What you eat and drink can affect the process of coronary heart disease in several ways:

- Fats and cholesterol: Reducing the total amount of fat you eat will reduce the amount of fats in your blood. Replacing some saturated fats and monounsaturated fats will help to improve the ratio of 'protective' cholesterol to 'harmful' cholesterol in your blood.

- Fruit and vegetables: Eating at least five portions of fruit and vegetables a day will reduce the risk of coronary heart disease, probably by helping to prevent atheroma from building up within the inside of the coronary arteries.

- Fish and fish oils: Eating oily fish two to three times a week may help to reduce the level of trigylcerides (fatty substances found in the blood) and prevent blood clots forming in the coronary arteries.

- Keeping a healthy weight: If you are overweight, reducing your weight will reduce the workload of your heart and help keep your blood pressure down.

- Salt: Reducing the amount of salt you eat will also help keep your blood pressure down.

- Alcohol: Too much alcohol can damage the heart muscle, increase blood pressure and also lead to weight gain.
- Eating fewer fats and reducing your cholesterol level: Cholesterol is a fatty substance which is mainly made in the body. The liver makes it from the saturated fats in food. The cholesterol enters the blood and is carried around by proteins. These combinations of cholesterol and proteins are called 'lipoproteins'. There are two main types of lipoprotein: low density lipoprotein (LDL) and high density lipoprotein (HDL). There is also a group of fatty substances in the blood called 'triglycerides'. Atheroma develops when LDL cholesterol undergoes a chemical process known as 'oxidation' and is taken up by cells in the coronary artery walls, where the narrowing process begins. On the other hand, HDL cholesterol removes cholesterol from the circulation and appears to protect against coronary heart disease. The ratio of HDL to LDL is therefore important. The goal is to have a low level of LDL and a high level of HDL. Eating a healthy diet can help to reduce your cholesterol level and improve your ratio of HDL to LDL cholesterol. It is possible to reduce the level of cholesterol in your blood by between 5 per cent and 10 per cent just by healthy eating. On average, a 1 per cent reduction in cholesterol can lower the risk of coronary heart disease by 2 per cent. Cholesterol is not found in large amounts in many foods, except for eggs and offal, such as liver and kidneys. The cholesterol in these foods does not usually make a great contribution to your blood cholesterol level but it is probably wise to limit eggs to about three a week. If you need to reduce your cholesterol level it is much more important to reduce the total fat content of your diet and to change the types of fat you eat. Eating a high-fibre diet may also help to reduce the amount of cholesterol that is absorbed from your intestine into the bloodstream.

- Choosing healthier fats: To reduce your cholesterol level you need to reduce the total amount of fat you eat and eat starchy foods instead (bread, pasta, rice, cereals and potatoes). Cut right down on saturated fats and substitute small amounts of polyunsaturated fats and monounsaturated fats for them.

- Eating more fruit and vegetables – and antioxidants: There is good evidence that eating a diet rich in a range of vegetables and fruits lowers the risk of heart disease. It is not known exactly why fruits and vegetables have this beneficial effect. It seems to be due to the antioxidants (vitamins and other substances) found in them. Antioxidants prevent 'oxidation' – the chemical process that enables cholesterol to form atheroma within the coronary artery walls. However, there is no evidence that taking vitamin tablets has the same effect. Fruits and vegetables are also rich in potassium, a mineral which may help to control blood pressure and prevent irregular heart rhythms. Fruits and green vegetables are also rich in folic acid. This reduces the blood level of a substance called homocysteine, which itself may be a risk factor for heart disease. Aim to eat at least five portions of fruit and vegetables a day. On average, people in the UK eat only three portions a day.

- Fish and fish oils: The oil in fish seems to reduce the risk of coronary heart disease by helping to lower blood trigylceride levels. Fish oils may also reduce the risk of blood clots forming because of the effect they have on cells in the blood called platelets. The particular oil in fish that has these beneficial effects is known as 'omega-3'. It is found mainly in oily fish such as herrings, kippers, mackerel, pilchards, sardines, salmon, fresh tuna, trout and anchovies.

Appendix V

Information from the Prostate Cancer Charity

- Prostate cancer is the cause of over 10,000 male deaths in the UK each year.
- Prostate cancer is the second most common cancer in men in the UK after lung cancer.
- Over 20,000 men are diagnosed with prostate cancer each year in the UK.
- The lifetime risk of developing prostate cancer is one in 12.
- Men with a family history of prostate cancer have an increased risk of developing the disease themselves.
- Prostate cancer is not confined to elderly men. Men as young as 40 can develop prostate cancer.
- Younger men are at higher risk of having aggressive prostate cancer.
- Prostate cancer occurs when the cells within the prostate gland begin to divide and grow in an uncontrolled manner. The cancerous gland then starts to grow larger and can press on the urethra. The cells then may break away, through the wall of the prostate gland and enter the surrounding tissue or travel throughout the body where they can grow and cause problems elsewhere, often in the bones.
- Prostate cancer is not related to Benign Prostatic Hyperplasia (BPH) which is a general non-malignant growth of the prostate gland that occurs in many older men.
- It is often impossible to distinguish between slow growing

tumours that cause no harm and fast growing tumours that kill.

- There are generally no symptoms associated with early prostate cancer. However, if and when they appear, the symptoms of prostate cancer and BPH are very similar. These include: difficulty or pain when passing urine, the need to pass urine more often, broken sleep due to increased visits to pass urine, waiting for long periods before the urine flows and the feeling that the bladder has not emptied fully.

- Other symptoms that can be associated with the later stage of the disease are: pain in the pelvis or loins, general bone pain and weight loss.

- There is no universally agreed preventative measure for prostate cancer, although diet and lifestyle are believed to be contributory factors.

Appendix VI

Extracted from: *No time to draw breath? What every smoker should know*. Published by Macmillan Cancer Relief

Lung Cancer in the UK – the facts:

- More than 40,000 new cases are identified each year
- 90 per cent of lung cancer cases are caused by smoking
- Not smoking or quitting makes a difference to your health
- The number of cases of lung cancer is rising – especially among women

The main group at risk of developing lung cancer are those who smoke, or who have smoked regularly in the past. It is never too late to give up smoking, and stopping now will greatly reduce your risk of getting lung cancer or heart disease in the future.

What to look out for:

If you have any of the following symptoms – especially if you smoke or have smoked in the past, you should go to your doctor for advice. But remember that often there is a simple explanation for such symptoms, so don't worry unnecessarily:

- A chest infection that doesn't get better
- Coughing up blood
- A cough that is changing or has been troubling you more
- Feeling more breathless than usual
- Chest pain

- Voice changes that last for more than three weeks, for example hoarseness
- Problems with swallowing
- Feeling generally unwell and tired

Information on stopping smoking

Telephone helplines

- England (Quitline) 0800 00 22 00
- Scotland (Smokeline) 0800 84 84 84
- Northern Ireland 028 9066 3281
- Wales 0325 697 500

- Your local health promotion unit can provide free information and advice on stopping smoking. Call your local health authority or health board or the freephone health information service on 0800 66 55 44.
- Your GP or health centre
- Your local pharmacist

Recommended Reading

The Anti-Aging Plan by Dr Marios Kyriazis, Element Books, 2000.

Come Alive by Beth MacEoin, Hodder & Stoughton, 2000.

Feel the Fear and Do It Anyway by Susan Jeffers, Hutchinson, 1987.

Manage Yourself, Manage your Life by Ian McDermott and Ian Shircore, Piatkus, 1999.

Mancare by Brian Ward, MacDonald, 1986.

The Naked Ape by Desmond Morris, Jonathan Cape, 1967.

The Optimum Nutrition Bible by Patrick Holford, Piatkus, 1997.

Panic Attacks by Christine Ingham, Thorsons Health Series, 2000.

The 7 Habits of Highly Effective People by Stephen R. Covey, Simon & Schuster, 1989.

The Sixty Minute Mother by Rob Parsons, Hodder & Stoughton, 2000.

Who Moved My Cheese? by Dr Spencer Johnson, Vermilion, 1999.

Index